10 Steps

to

Connecting

with Your

Customers

DARTNELL is a publisher serving the world of business with books, manuals, newsletters and bulletins, and training materials for executives, managers, supervisors, salespeople, financial officials, personnel executives, and office employees. Dartnell also produces management and sales training videos and audiocassettes, publishes many useful business forms, and many of its materials and films are available in languages other than English. Dartnell, established in 1917, serves the world's business community. For details, catalogs, and product information, write to:

THE DARTNELL CORPORATION
4660 N Ravenswood Ave
Chicago, IL 60640-4595, U.S.A.
or phone (800) 621-5463 in U.S. and Canada

Dartnell Training Limited
125 High Holborn
London, England
WC1V 6QA
or phone 011-44-071-404-1585

Copyright 1995
William Bethel

Library of Congress Catalog Card Number: 94-068812

ISBN 0–85013–201–0

Printed in the United States of America by the
Dartnell Press, Chicago, IL 60640-4595

To Aileen, Christopher, Fiona,
Michael, and Flannery

ABOUT THE AUTHOR

Bill Bethel is a nationally recognized, award-winning speaker and business consultant who has given more than 3000 speeches and seminars in his career. He has been contributing to the bottom line of his clients and receiving rave reviews for their improved performance. He has trained and inspired thousands of salespeople to achieve their share of the American dream.

For more information on speeches and seminars contact: The Dartnell Speakers Bureau (800) 545-7550.

ACKNOWLEDGMENTS

To all the people who have helped me learn to connect with other people. I would especially like to acknowledge Eleanor Dugan for her expertise and care in sending this manuscript through charm school. Without her, it would not be what it is. Also, special thanks go to Vera Derr, my editor at Dartnell, and to Shannon Schadler for her typing, suggestions, organization, and, most of all, her patience. And, for her support and understanding, I want to give my most heartfelt thanks to my wife and business partner, Sheila. She is the one who makes it all worthwhile.

TABLE OF CONTENTS

PREFACE

When I was a kid working my way through college, my first sales job was selling encyclopedias door to door. My sales manager told me that when I rang the doorbell and customers answered, I had ten seconds to make a decision. Should I be aggressive and "shove the product down their throat?" Or should I should play the role of a shy and timid person, stumble in my speech, and solicit their help? Pretty awful advice, either way!

In today's fast-changing, highly competitive market, we must communicate an entirely different message: *partnership*. We must demonstrate concern for and a real desire to serve the customer. To do this, we need a complete understanding of sensitive, superior, and service-targeted communication techniques. We need to know the 10 steps that help us connect with our customers.

1. Understand your message (What message is sent?)
2. Listen intently (Do you know what I mean?)
3. Ask questions (Do I understand what you're saying?)
4. Speak clearly (How do you say it?)
5. Cross the barriers (How do you overcome culture, gender, and age considerations?)
6. Use influence and persuasion (How do you use friendly persuasion?)
7. Negotiate (How do you get what you want?)
8. Use technology (Is there another way to do this?)

9. Use body language (What silent messages are you sending?)
10. Use self-talk (How do you communicate with yourself?)

I'm excited to share with you what I have learned about communication while training tens of thousands of salespeople and from talking with other sales experts about how sales communication has changed over the last four decades.

Communication comes from the Latin word communicatus, which means "to make common." That's my objective in this book—to make common the best of a variety of communication skills as they apply to sales situations in which you find yourself every day. I want to help you sell more and increase your production, your volume, and your market share. I want you to keep the customer coming back over and over again.

I also want you to feel more competent because competence breeds confidence. When you feel more confident, you will try new ideas, be more creative, and tap into your special talents. This, in turn, increases your competence, which then continues to increase your confidence. Communication skills are essential to your personal cycle of competence, confidence, and results.

In this book, we are going to discuss the skills, techniques, and attitudes that will make you a great salesperson by allowing you to understand how two-way communication leads to sales success.

There's an African legend about a remarkable bird that could build a perfect nest. All the other birds wanted to know how she did it, and they asked her to explain. First, she said, "I collect some mud." One of the birds said,

"Oh, yes, I understand," and flew off. She continued, "Then I gather twigs and leaves." Another bird said, "Now I understand," and left. As she described each step, yet another bird would decide it now knew how to build the perfect nest and would fly away. Finally, when she got to the last crucial step there was no one left.

The moral is, stay with this book to the end. As you read, open your eyes, ears, mind, and heart. Use your experience to confirm what you already know. Use your intellect to learn more. Use your feelings to expand your beliefs. Then apply these lessons when you make your next sales call. And the one after that. And the one after that. Keep practicing until you truly communicate with your customer.

STEP ONE

UNDERSTAND YOUR MESSAGE (WHAT MESSAGE IS SENT?)

A salesman was standing in front of 100 people, making a group presentation. Suddenly, as he made his most crucial point, the sound system started making terrible squawking noises. A maintenance man was summoned. The man took off the back of the amplifier and poked around. Finally he turned to the waiting audience and announced, "I think this speaker has a screw loose."

Sometimes your potential customers may feel the same way about you, even when you're not using a microphone. How do you persuade them to exchange their money for your product or service? How do you design a sales talk that is in sync with both your personal image and your product's image? You start by understanding the philosophy and process of effective communication so you can appeal to your customer's minds and hearts, their hopes and dreams, their cares and concerns.

Good sales communication has three parts:
1. The messenger;
2. The message; and
3. The method.

The messenger is you. The message is the information about your product or service. The method is your technique of delivering that information.

THE MESSENGER

The messenger and the message are often difficult to separate. Obviously you are not your product, but, in the customer's mind, you and what you sell are almost interchangeable. Your first job as the messenger is to develop a sense of harmony with your product and to reflect its positive aspects.

I believe that people buy from people they like. Or, at least, they buy from people they respect and trust. How do you approach other people? Do you focus on what makes them different from you or on what makes you alike? Your best approach is to emphasize your similarities. People do business with people they like, and they usually like people who are similar to them in some way. I call these my "A" clients. These A clients are the ones with whom I can communicate easily because they like me. When people like me, they usually want to agree with me, and if they agree with me, I certainly like them.

It's almost always true that the higher a product's price, the more important you, the salesperson, are in the sales process. Of course, people prefer to buy a competitively priced, quality product, but, when all else is equal, they prefer to buy it from people they like.

When I vote, I vote for the people who agree most with my beliefs and who, I feel, won't change their position as soon as they take office. I want to trust these people. When I buy a product, I buy it from the salesperson or company that I feel is going to care the most about what is good for me now and after the sale. Again, I want to trust them. No matter how good the message is, if the person delivering the message doesn't convince me that I will receive all of the promised benefits, I simply don't buy.

So you truly are both the messenger and the message. Your style, image, and reputation are as important as the words you say or how you say them.

THE WHO-WHAT-HOW EVALUATION

We connect with our customers not only through words but through facial expressions, gestures, energy level, wardrobe, grooming, tone of voice, confidence, and attention to the customer—everything we do throughout the sales process projects a message to our customers. To understand what kind of message we're sending, we first have to know ourselves. Once we do, our actions will automatically reflect and communicate exactly who we are, what we do, and how the customer can best benefit from our product or service. This is the Who-What-How evaluation.

Who Are You? What unique perspective do you bring to this selling situation? There's an old story about a man who was asked to identify himself at a bank before they would cash his check. He pulled out a mirror, looked at it, and said, "Yes, that's definitely me." It's easy to identify yourself when you're looking in a mirror, but it's much harder to identify the real self behind your surface image. Ask yourself:

- What are my skills?
- What are my abilities?
- What are my talents?
- What are my strengths?
- What are my weaknesses?
- What are my prejudices?
- What are my likes?
- What are my dislikes?
- What are my desires?
- What things in my emotional make-up, physical presence, and experience will benefit my customer?

When you know the answers to these questions, you can bring a unique perspective to your selling communications.

What Do You Do? I know you can sell. But did you know that you can actually sell more by focusing less on making the sale and more on solving your customers' problems, servicing their needs, and making them feel important? When you communicate your interest in them, you have a much better chance of convincing your buyers they will be better off by doing business with you. For example, you can make yourself invaluable because of your expertise in production techniques, the intricacies of import-export paperwork, the most efficient way to ship the product, or creative ways to use the service.

As your awareness of your customers increases, so will your sales. Awareness builds knowledge, and knowledge is power. The more you know, the better you can communicate. The better you communicate, the more you connect with your customer.

How Can You Benefit Your Customer? Are you adept at spotting the real benefits to and buying motivations for each customer? You undoubtedly know about communicating all the *features* and *benefits* of a product, but do you have the persistence, perception, and sometimes sixth sense to identify and appeal to the *personal motivations* associated with your product or service?

- **Features** are what your product is: "An electronic translator the size of a credit card, with a 40,000-word vocabulary and word-search capabilities."
- **Benefits** are what your product does: "It translates English to Spanish and Spanish to English at the touch of a button."
- **Personal Motivations** translate features and benefits into what the product can do for the customer: "When you're traveling in Spanish-speaking countries, you will never again feel foolish or helpless."

EXPLOITING MOTIVATIONS

At a meeting I attended recently, an advertising director was presenting a new product and was focusing only on its features. As he described feature after feature, I watched all the experienced salespeople slowly turn off. It was obvious from their facial expressions they were bored and thinking about something else. Why? Because experienced salespeople know that features are only a third of the equation in a sale. What they wanted to know was: What does this product do (benefits)? What will it mean to my customers (motivation)?

The advertising director, by concentrating on features, was ignoring the points the listeners felt were most important. His presentation got little response because he ignored benefits and motivations.

On the other hand, Joy Johnson, the sales manager of Loew's Ventana Canyon Resort in Arizona, is terrific at spotting motivations. She told me that she has learned to listen carefully for her customers' real motivations. One was looking for a site for a large convention. As she was explaining the features and benefits of the resort, he kept asking questions about their golf course. It was obvious that his primary motivation was not the business meeting, but a round of golf. Joy quickly focused on the golf course, explaining a unique feature: There were lights that permitted golfing at night.

Her prospect was clearly intrigued, saying "I've never heard of night golf, but I'd sure like to try it." That point was the "what's in it for me" motivation that closed the sale. By listening for the prospects' points of view and motivations, Joy remains one of the top salespeople in the resort industry.

DEVELOPING YOUR SKILLS

One of the best definitions I have ever heard for sales communication is "fostering understanding between the buyer and the seller." This happens when you transfer the knowledge and opinions in your head and heart to the heads and hearts of your buyers. You do this with communication skills.

A skill is any ability you use to achieve a successful conclusion with little conscious thought. In other words, it's something you can do in your sleep. When Michelangelo was asked to paint the Sistine Chapel ceiling, he'd never painted an enormous space like that before. He knew the logistics would be formidable, but he also knew that he had developed all the *skills* necessary for the job. When you communicate clearly, concisely, and completely, you can change the way people think, feel, and act. You don't just *communicate*, you communicate *effectively*. You need to make each of the ten steps described in this book so automatic that you don't have to think about them.

Here's an example. Describe a popular American breakfast. You might answer, "The upper part of a chemically preserved porcine haunch and the ova of domesticated birds." Or you could say, "Ham and eggs." To be understood and to understand what is said is real communication. People often say things they don't actually mean and mean things they don't actually say. The English language is full of opportunities for misunderstanding. A salesperson was demonstrating a new computer that was supposed to translate spoken English into written computer files. He confidently told the computer, "This new display can recognize speech." The client waited while the message was printed out and was astonished to read, "This nudist play can wreck a nice beach." Maybe you're not communicating what you intend. Maybe sometimes you're misunderstood.

BUILDING YOUR PRODUCT KNOWLEDGE

Some years ago I was consulting with a company that sold limited partnership interests in California apartment houses. Because of the strict securities laws, the company insisted that each salesperson tell exactly the same story. To ensure this, the company created a 30-minute promotional video for each salesperson to show to prospects. All the salesperson needed was an electrical outlet and an order book.

One stormy January afternoon, salesperson Linda Marx arrived for an appointment with a pension fund manager, a man she believed had the authority to make a substantial investment. Just as she started her presentation, the power went out. So much for the video demonstration. But Linda knew how to sell, and she knew her product information. She asked her prospect to step to the window where they would have more light so she could show him why he should consider the investment. Linda pulled out a yellow pad and a pen and gave her sales pitch while she drew illustrations, key words, graphs, and charts on her pad. She made the biggest sale of her career.

Your customers want to know that you really know what you're talking about and selling. It's hard to trust someone who has to keep shuffling papers and looking things up. Know your product!

THE MESSAGE

With the first few words you say, an image forms in your customers' minds that will almost inevitably lead them to accept or reject you and your product. What opening statement, question, or action will create a favorable impression? Here are some possibilities:

> "May I show you a way to cut your advertising budget by 5 percent *and* increase your sales 5 percent at the same time?"

> "People in your position are always looking for new ideas. I have one that will increase your productivity without increasing your costs."

> "Look out your window at that revolving sign on top of my car. Wouldn't that grab the attention of passing motorists if it were here on the corner of your used car lot?"

First impressions count. What message do your appearance and actions give in those first few minutes? Let me give you an example. I recently took my Jaguar to the dealership for repairs very early one morning. I had to wait a few minutes for the owner to arrive and open up. When he did arrive, he was driving a Chrysler. What did that say to me about his commitment to my Jaguar? Not much.

On the other hand, a life insurance salesman contacted me not long ago to sell me additional insurance. I told him I had two large policies, maybe more than I needed. He didn't say anything, just reached in his briefcase and pulled out eight different insurance policies that he had purchased on his own life over the last 15 years. They totaled $1.5 million. Then he said, "May I take just a few moments to explain why I've built this insurance portfolio?" Even though I didn't want to buy insurance, I was impressed that he had bought his own product.

Do you own or use your product? How do you communicate your belief in your product or service? Do you drive the car that you're selling? Do you purchase your clothes in the store where you work? Do you live in the neighborhood where you sell houses? I once ran a training program for Apple Computer, and 12 of the 15 people in my audience were taking notes on Apple Notebooks. They believed in their product.

WHAT IS YOUR MISSION MESSAGE?

Why do you, as a salesperson, exist? Why does your company exist? What is the primary purpose that drives you to sell this particular product? I sell consulting, speeches, seminars, audio and videotapes, and books that I hope convey information and inspiration to my listeners and readers. My mission is to show that everybody can learn to be more successful, have a better personal life, and truly make a difference in the lives of other people. But my mission can only be accomplished if I can help people develop the attitudes and aptitudes necessary for success. My purpose is to make available as much of the beneficial information I have to as many people as I can.

WHAT IS YOUR OBJECTIVE MESSAGE?

What are you going for? What are your long-term and short-term goals? What is your goal for this particular sales contact? Are these objectives in harmony with your company's objectives? With your customer's objectives? My personal objective is less altruistic than my mission.

My long-term objective is to create information products that distributors can sell and thus create future income for the time when I stop delivering speeches and seminars. My short-term objective is to create enough current income to enable me to pursue my long-term objective and my mission. My objective for any single sales contact is to help my customers achieve their goals so they will help me achieve mine.

WHAT IS YOUR VALUE MESSAGE?

Are you selling quality? Service? Economy? Convenience? What are you willing to compromise in order to lower the price, and what won't or can't you compromise on? Would you lower the quality of your product or service to lower the price? Or would you be willing to delay delivery to keep the quality high? Is on-time delivery more important than price or quality?

Not too long ago I was hiring a handyman to do some work around my house. He said he'd rather charge by the project than the hour. I agreed and explained the jobs I wanted done. He took out his pencil, calculated everything, and said the total would be $800. I looked shocked and flinched, which is my standard negotiating stance. "That's more than I can afford right now," I said. He said, "What about $600?" I said I really had about $400 in mind. He agreed to this price. I didn't know if I should feel good about my negotiating ability or bad because I hadn't negotiated even more. Had he doubled his real price to give himself a bargaining cushion? Or was I cheating him? Did he use lower-quality materials or do some of the repairs in a slapdash manner? I was initially content, but later I wondered about his value message.

From my point of view, it was worth $400 not to spend several days on a ladder replacing light fixtures, mending fences, and so on. But it wasn't worth $800. That's an example of value versus price. From the handyman's point of view, it was worth compromising to get the job.

What is your value message? How and what are you willing to compromise? Do you stand firm with your price, or are you and your company ready to cut and compromise? If you cut your prices to get orders, how do you make up the difference? Or do you prefer to demonstrate increased value to your customers and refuse to compromise on price? If push came to shove, which factors would you be willing to compromise on: quality, timely delivery, service, or price? Do these compromises conflict with your mission or objectives?

WHAT DO YOUR CUSTOMERS BUY?

Quickly answer this question: Have you ever bought a *thing*? I don't believe I have. Now, don't misunderstand. I accept delivery of things and I often carry them home from stores, but I've never actually bought one.

- Just yesterday I purchased an ice cream cone. I didn't want the ice cream or the cone. What I wanted was the pleasure of the cool sweetness contrasting with the crunchy texture, the nostalgia of childhood memories, of desires fulfilled in the perfection of a sunny afternoon.
- I'm a compulsive book buyer. Do I really want the pages of print in a binding? No. I want the expectation of exciting hours spent in another

reality or of new knowledge that will give me power over some part of my life.

- I drive a Jaguar. Did I buy it so I could speed at 140 miles per hour while spending a fortune on payments and maintenance? Does it actually allow me to get anywhere faster or better in today's traffic? No, but I've convinced myself that it's the best-looking car on the road. By extension, it feeds my ego because people turn to look, parking attendants treat me with deference, and I just feel good sitting in it.

So don't try to sell me *things*. Sell me ideas, concepts, and feelings. Sell me pride, pleasure, satisfaction, and self-esteem.

WHY DO YOUR CUSTOMERS BUY?

The wisdom and excellence of any purchase is unimportant compared to the buyer's feelings. What would you feel if you were given the following sales presentation?

Do you travel a lot? Do you fly? Then maybe you'd like to consider a lifetime pass on my airline. Imagine all the benefits. You can tell your friends that you'll never have to buy an airplane ticket again. Just flash your pass and get on board. Even the strangers standing in line to buy tickets will be impressed. Obviously, since you travel frequently and almost exclusively with us, you're going to be treated royally. We will pamper you whenever you're on board. We'll upgrade you to first class whenever possible. We'll send you free tickets so your spouse or business associates can accompany you. But, most important, if you're now flying more than 20 coast to coast trips each year, you'll cut your costs 50 percent by buying a lifetime pass. Can you think of any reason why you wouldn't want to be pampered at half the cost?

This salesperson is trying to sell you ideas, concepts, feelings, pride, pleasure, and savings—not movement from one place to another. If you communicate these things to your customers, you'll have their attention and interest, stimulate their desires, and motivate them to take action.

WHAT DO YOUR CUSTOMERS WANT?

I believe that customers want salespeople to get down to business quickly. But how can you get to the point without skipping the necessary preliminary steps: building rapport, identifying and understanding customers' problems and needs, and getting them to agree that there is a problem that needs to be solved?

Today's buyers are interested in cost, on-time delivery, quality service, and confidence in the company. Most important, they want solutions to their real problems. Use your communication skills to show you understand your prospects' problems, needs, and wants. Throw away extraneous issues and go straight to the core ideas that are important to buyers. Convince them that you have something special to offer that they cannot purchase as easily or safely from anyone else. Show them how you can solve their problems, fix what's wrong, and help to achieve their desires. That's what sells and that's what you should be communicating.

THE SEVEN CUSTOMER'S QUESTIONS

There are seven questions in every customer's mind that you must answer to move them through the sales process.

1. Will I talk to this salesperson?
2. Will I listen with an open mind?
3. Do I *need* the benefits of this product or service?
4. Does this product or service give me the benefits I want?
5. Is this salesperson the best source for this product or service?
6. Is the price reasonable?
7. Why should I buy from this person now?

These questions, often unspoken, must be answered. Your job as a good sales communicator is to offer answers that will encourage, enlighten, and excite your customers to form favorable opinions. They need to decide that you are there to help them achieve their desires.

When you know what you stand for and what your objective is—that is, why you exist—and you communicate this effectively, you develop respect and trust. It is always easier to communicate and make a sale when you are respected and trusted.

THE METHOD

In the final analysis, we are all trying to sell our ideas, opinions, and beliefs to other people. We accomplish this by expecting them to buy, encouraging them to buy, and explaining how they can buy.

We persuade our customers to buy, first by skillful questioning that encourages them to tell us their own expectations and then by suggesting the steps they can take to solve problems or fulfill needs. Finally, we *must* explain the process for confirming acceptance, setting a delivery date, filling out an order form, and/or making out a check. This may seem too elementary to bother with, but an amazing number of potential customers don't buy because they're not sure what to do next. If customers are confused or uncertain about this process, they won't buy.

THE MAGIC MINUTE

Your "Magic Minute" is the first minute that you're in contact with a customer. You can get a consistent response when you are consistent in your approach. What happens that first minute can be more important than anything you say or do in the subsequent 30 minutes. In fact, if the start isn't right, you may not get 30 minutes.

Prospects' first impressions come from your visual appearance, the words you use, and the feelings you convey. When they are favorably impressed, they will probably listen to what you have to say. If they are not favorably impressed, then everything you say and do after the Magic Minute must be directed at overcoming the barriers in their minds. Your approach in that first minute is one of the most important parts of effective sales communication.

People in today's world are used to the 60-second "soundbite." Many advertisers have even found that a 30-second spot sells just as well, and vivid 10-second commercials can be as effective as 30-second ones. All day long we routinely react almost instantly to television blurbs, newspaper headlines, magazine ads, and even letters and brochures that come in the mail. Each of these methods of communicating must grab our attention, stimulate our interest, and create desires, often in ten seconds or less.

Time is your enemy and your friend.

How many times has a prospect said, "Tell him I can't see him today, I just haven't got the time;" or "Tell her I'm not available right now. If she gets me on the phone I won't get off for an hour." Most people are so busy that they simply avoid listening to a salesperson unless that person's first few words sell them on the potential value of exchanging their precious time for information. That's your job. Your first words should tell prospects exactly why you are there and why it's worth their while to talk with you.

Ask yourself:
- What is the single best statement that will lead me to what I want from this customer?
- What is the next best statement I can use that will relate to the needs and interests of my customer?
- What statement can I use that will specifically get the customer's attention, attract his or her interest, and entice his or her desire?
- How can I edit my remarks so that all of these things will be achieved in 60 seconds or less?

When you can answer these questions, you have your 60-second soundbite.

We live in a world where everybody is looking for a quick fix. The successful sales communicator understands potential buyers' impatience, respects their time, and gets to the point as rapidly as possible. That is the only way to establish a warm relationship, to move to the next step of the sales process, or to close the sale and get the order.

YOUR OPENING STATEMENT

Your first words identify you and your desire to help the customer. They also start to create rapport with the prospect. Often they refer to something you have in common with this particular customer. Even if you've never met before, there may still be some connection. It could be the letter or telephone call you used to make the appointment, or the friend who referred you. If possible, phrase your opening statement in a questioning form, such as:

- Did Jim tell you I was going to call?
- Have there been any major changes in your business since the last time we spoke?
- How can I help you today?

Your opening statement should get your customers' attention. There's no better way to do this than to ask a question. A question usually requires an answer. Your prospect must think, formulate a response, and become an active part of the selling process.

Your questions and comments should focus your customers' attention on your product or service in a favorable manner, but remember that your customers are interested in their own problems, not yours. They want solutions, they want help, and they want to be important to you. Focus your questions on them. Win their interest with questions like:

- What is the biggest concern in your business right now?
- What would help you to do your job better?
- If you could redesign this department, what problems would you tackle first?

When prospects answer these fact-finding questions, you've automatically captured their interest.

Most people tune out anything that sounds remotely like a sales pitch. Communicate naturally so you can break through the barriers most customers set up in a sales situation. Cultivate an eager "me too" response instead of a wary "so what?" If you can get your customer to identify and say, "Me too," you have connected. If they say, "So what?," you haven't.

YOUR HOOK

What is the most interesting thing you can say or do to capture your prospect's attention? In other words, what is your *hook*? Newspapers use headlines; television and radio use promotional teasers; magazines use titles. These are all attention-getting hooks. What hook will you use to get your customer's attention?

Some hooks are visual, instead of verbal. My friend Alan Parisse, a professional speaker, is only 5'4" tall. When he begins his program, he walks over to the lectern, stands behind it, frowns, walks off stage, returns with a plastic box, sets it down, and steps up on it so the audience can see him. Before he says a word, he has the group in the palm of his hand, laughing and ready to accept whatever he has to say.

Another friend of mine sells humorous greeting cards to stationery stores. Just before he walks into the store, he slips on a red rubber clown nose. Does he get attention? You bet. I also have heard of a real estate salesman who carries a "For Sale" sign under his arm wherever he goes. He doesn't have to say anything. People are always asking him questions about their real estate. Can you develop a visual hook in your sales approach?

"WHAT'S IN IT FOR ME?"

Many salespeople use a humorous anecdote or a personal story to build rapport. It's important that this story focuses on the customer, not the salesperson. If you use such a story, be sure it relates to the customer's personal interests. Try to make it answer the unspoken question: "What's in it for me?"

Yes, you want to communicate business advantages and solutions, but do it on a personal level. No matter what they say, people invariably make buying decisions based on personal motivations. Even when they are purchasing for their company, the final decision still reflects some perceived personal benefit.

This *doesn't* mean a bribe or a kickback. The rewards for choosing one product over another can include increased power, control, time, confidence, prestige, creativity, and so on, or decreased uncertainty, stress, headaches, problems, frustrations, loss, fear, and so forth.

Directly or indirectly, show the decision makers what's in it for them. Answer that question, and you've probably made the sale.

Basic:	*This machine shells 4,000 nuts per hour.*
Better:	*With this high-speed shelling machine, you can't get behind in your production schedule. That ought to get the district manager off your back! You'd really like that, wouldn't you? And you'll have more time for hands-on merchandising and designing new confections. Are those your two biggest priorities right now?*

Questions allow you to constantly reconfirm the customer's opinions, beliefs, and priorities.

FROM PACING TO CONNECTING

Pacing is your first step to connecting with your customer. Pacing starts with mirroring. That means that you match or mirror the mood, voice tone, stance, and gestures of your customer. Most people do this unconsciously, but you can also train yourself to observe and imitate. Remember the old saying, "Misery loves company?" Well, cheerfulness loves cheerfulness, eagerness loves eagerness, and success loves success. Excitement, enthusiasm, achievement, knowledge, and action all love their counterpart.

Successful salespeople often have a highly developed ability to mirror the moods of their customers. In pacing, once they are in harmony with their customer, they slowly change to a mood that is more favorable to successfully concluding the sales interview. As they change, their customer usually changes with them.

Start by matching your prospects vocally and visually until, subconsciously, they have decided that you are like them. Then adjust your pacing and lead them to agree with you.

Pacing really works—most of the time. Sometimes it helps the pacer as much as the pacee. I like my friend Len a lot, but Len is a slow thinker. He's extremely bright and highly educated, but his pattern is to ponder things carefully before he speaks. Now, I've got what some call a fast mind. Usually, after a few words, I can anticipate what the speaker is going to say. Unfortunately, this is *not* a strength! It's a weakness. Especially when I'm talking with Len. I might ask him, "How's it going at work?" and he'll say something like, "Well, ... work ... is ... fine.... We, ... um, ... started ... a new ... project ... and ... I've been ... put ... in charge.... I guess ... it will ... work ... out okay."

AAAGH! By that time, if I can force myself to let him get that far, I'm going crazy. Usually, I've anticipated what I think he's going to say, and I find myself interrupting. I try hard not to, try to force myself to relax and match his pace, but so far I haven't succeeded 100 percent. Pacing can be hard work.

Connecting means you advance from simple pacing to a more emotional level. You touch your customers' hearts as well as their intellects. Often we connect when we talk about universal truths, feelings, and gut reactions. For example, "I think I know how you feel. I also want to make a difference in this world. That's why I'm excited about this product. It does a great deal for the environment without sacrificing production or profits."

Both pacing and connecting establish trust. When you mirror your customers' actions, they see themselves in you. This may sound like manipulation, but it's not. Everyone does it all the time. I was walking with my mother the other day. She's 84 years old. Did I walk down the street at my normal pace? No, I matched her pace.

When I'm selling to a busy person who functions at a very frantic level, do I spend 15 minutes talking about the weather, his golf game, and my vacation? No, I get down to business immediately and match his method of processing information. I meet him on his level and then, when I have aroused his attention, interest, and desire to know more, I am able to slow down our exchange and lead him to a more measured gait.

IDENTIFYING THE BEST APPROACH

Many people say seeing is believing, but few say the same about hearing or doing. However, all three are true. Psychologists use the term "neuro-linguistic programming" to explain how people process information visually, auditorially, and kinesthetically. Seeing is the visual, hearing is the auditory, and movement in physical space is the kinesthetic. We process information all three ways, but most people favor one method. And to be effective communicators, we need to be in harmony with the prospect's dominant mode of the moment.

That's a real problem at our house because I am almost totally auditory and my wife is almost totally visual. If you want to give me directions to visit you, don't draw me a map, just explain it to me. If I hear it, I can do it. My wife is just the opposite. If you give her verbal directions ("Go west on Main Street and take the second right after the third traffic light.") she will never arrive. But give her a map, and she can find anything.

Most people alternate between the three ways of processing information. Look for clues about a prospect's primary or current method of communication. Have you heard someone say, "That looks good to me," or "That sounds interesting," or "That feels about right, but we have a long way to go?" These are clues that the prospect may be most receptive to information in a visual, verbal, or tactile/spatial form. Sometimes you need to ask questions and listen to the answers to help you decide your customer's dominant process of communicating at that moment.

Some questions you might ask would be:

"I want to make sure I'm seeing this right. Could you illustrate how you do that? Paint me the bigger picture." (visual)

"Could you explain that to me in more detail?" (verbal)

"I may be confused. Can you demonstrate how that would work?" (kinesthetic)

Then decide from the response if your guess was correct. If not, adjust your approach.

"I can see this system changing the whole look of this office. Your new workstation would be over there ... " (visual)

"There are five advantages to this change. Let's go over them ... " (verbal)

"You're really cramped here, I can see, and you'd like to spread your operations into new areas ... " (kinesthetic)

Good salespeople listen for the clues that help them get in sync with their customer. All of these techniques are important, and they will help you make a successful sale.

Good communicators influence decisions by building a common ground with the customer, using neuro-linguistic techniques for better understanding, and appealing to motivations.

IDENTIFYING MOTIVATIONS

People buy because they believe they will be better off after they exchange their money for your service or product. There are five basic motivators that you should be aware of when you are connecting with your customer. These motivators are both positive and negative. People desire gain and fear loss. Surprisingly, people are more eager to prevent loss than they are to create gain. Think about that. Even though we all enjoy winning, we certainly don't want to lose.

Here are the five basic motivators that cause people to buy:

1. Profit. People want gain, achievement, or a benefit of some sort.

2. Peace of mind. Fear of loss is a major motivator. People want to protect what they have, save time, and avoid aggravation. They want a service that protects their interests, a product that lasts. All these factors contribute to peace of mind.

3. Pleasure. Pleasure can be comfort, convenience, enjoyment, affection, admiration, luxury, or good health. It can emphasize youth, beauty, or sexual attraction. There is a heavy emphasis on pleasure appeals in our society.

4. Pain. Most people want protection from pain, loss, conflict, and embarrassment, even from plain old hard work. Can you help your customer avoid pain by making his or her job easier?

5. Pride. Pride includes anything that lets someone say, "I am special." Everyone wants to be admired, approved of, appreciated, and accepted. Feeling important is one of the most basic buyer motivators.

Design your approach so that your first question or statement shows which of the five motivators your product or service is most likely to appeal to. Make your questions or comments as numerous and varied as you can. Study your prospects and their surroundings and look for clues to their interests. Then listen.

It's easy to get so wrapped up in your presentations that you almost ignore your prospects, but *don't*. Be sure your product knowledge and presentation have become instinctive so that you can focus on the prospect's comments and body language. And do your homework before you meet with your prospect. Personal and company background, combined with what you observe, can help you determine the real buying motives.

DECIDING ON YOUR OBJECTIVES

At the beginning of every selling situation, you should know or try to guess the answers to four questions:

- What is your objective in this selling situation?
- Why are you talking to this customer?
- What is the prospect's real objective?
- Why is he or she listening to you?

When you know the answers, include them in your presentation as often as possible, and use them to lead you to the result you want: "Mr. Smith, now that we know your objective is to speed up the time between the warehouse and the loading dock, I can demonstrate how our low-maintenance conveyor-belt system will do this for you faster and cheaper than hand-trucking." In just one sentence you have communicated that you understand his objectives and that you have a product he should buy.

How do you define your objectives in a selling situation? One of the techniques I've used is to write out a statement before my sales calls:

This sales call will be successful if the customer _____ _____ .

Most people would write, "Close the sale." That may be true much of the time, but sometimes the answer is that the customer agrees to go on to the next step in the sales process: "I like what you've told me. Leave your literature so my engineers can study it and give me a call next Tuesday." Or, if the customer says, "I really liked the preliminary information. Would you write up a proposal outlining all the details and specifications as well as delivery dates, costs, and financial terms? I'll present it at the next board meeting." That progress in the sales process may more than meet your objective for that call. Clarify your objectives so you know when you've won!

STRESS PROBLEM SOLVING

As you approach your prospects, ask questions and observe what's going on around you. Discover your customers' problems and concerns by listening with your eyes, ears, and heart, as well as your intellect. Then restate prospects' concerns and ask if you've understood them correctly. Continue this nonconfrontational questioning until you are sure your prospects are aware of their problems and are eager for a solution. Only then should you offer your product or service as a way to deal with the problem.

Here's an example: "Are your customers having a hard time finding the temporary entrance with the street outside dug up?" That sounds like a simple question. But that question and the answer to it resulted in $6,200 in sales for a sign salesperson. She was driving through a strange neighborhood and noticed that the streets and sidewalks were being ripped up. She stopped immediately and cold-canvassed the businesses on these streets, asking if their customers were having trouble parking and finding their temporary entrances. "Yes," the store owners told her, "that's a big problem." The stores were losing business, but they hadn't figured out what to do. She immediately sold them signs that apologized for the inconvenience and directed customers to temporary store entrances and parking.

Remember Henry Hill, the salesman hero of the Broadway show *The Music Man*? He sold musical instruments and band uniforms in small Iowa towns. Not a very big market, but he knew that if he could create or discover a need that he could fill, then he could make a sale. Early in the show, he sings a song called "Trouble in River City," pointing out the disaster that a pool hall could cause in the community. This "unwholesome" influence, he warns, could endanger the morals of the children and the entire town. Professor Hill firmly establishes this potential disaster in the minds of his listeners, and only then does he move on to a solution: a town band. "How," he asks, "could any pool table ever hope to compete with a gold trombone?" Of course, he is able to solve the citizens' problem by selling them band instruments and uniforms.

This is a perfect example of how to present a sales proposition to your clients. First a problem and then a solution. If the specter of a pool hall hadn't suggested potential danger, the townspeople would have felt no need for a band as a healthful alternative.

When salespeople fail, it's usually because they have tried to communicate solutions before the prospect was clear about the problems. If a doctor prescribed medicine for you before an examination, it would probably be considered malpractice. The same is true in sales. You wouldn't trust a doctor who never asked how you felt. Or a mechanic who didn't say, "What seems to be the problem?" Or an attorney who didn't want to know why you had decided to consult her. Salespeople are professionals and should ask questions just like other professionals.

Good sales communicators are problem solvers. Show that you can solve, fix, and help. Identify your prospects' needs and wants clearly, then show them you are willing to serve those needs and wants. How do you do that? It's simple.

IDENTIFYING PROBLEMS

1. You ask. Asking is a major part of communication. But after you ask you must use another communication technique.
2. You listen. Keep quiet and really listen to what the prospect says.
3. You speak. Restate the point to be sure that you understand and that the prospect *knows* you understand.
4. Even when you're listening, let your body speak. Nod, shrug, gesture, use pacing. Show that you're alive, well, and in the same place as your listener.

All this shows your prospects that you care about them. They feel important because you are truly communicating.

BECOMING YOUR CUSTOMER'S ALLY

Zig Zigler, the well-known motivational speaker, says, "The way to get everything you want is to help others get everything they want." If you can communicate your eagerness to do this, you are halfway to success. The second half is achieved by communicating exactly how you will help them achieve their goals.

Frank Betcher, author of *How I Raised Myself From Failure to Success in Sales*, said, "Just show people what they want and how they can get it and you will be a success." In other words, your job as a sales communicator is to create pictures in your customers' minds of solutions to their spoken and unspoken problems.

COMMUNICATION'S ROLE

Former president Gerald Ford said that if he could go back to school, he "would spend more time learning to listen, to speak, and to write effectively, for communication is the basis of all success." Lee Iacocca, former chairman of Chrysler Corporation, said, "The ability to communicate is everything." If achievers like these two men believe so strongly in the power of communication, maybe you should be willing to devote some time to perfecting your sales communication skills.

Here's a warning: Good communication skills do *not* replace basic selling skills. Communication strengthens and enhances selling skills, and makes them more powerful, but you can never get away from the primary selling steps:

1. Get attention.
2. Build rapport.
3. Discover needs and problems.
4. State benefits and solutions.
5. Answer objections.
6. Ask for the order.
7. Close the sale.

This book is about the communication skills you'll need to accomplish these seven steps. Much of the emphasis will be on methods and techniques, but the text will also emphasize you, the messenger.

STEP TWO

LISTEN INTENTLY (DO YOU KNOW WHAT I MEAN?)

A man was driving down the road when a cop pulled him over and said, "Did you know that your wife fell out of the car about a mile back?"

The man looked up at the sky, folded his hands, and said, "Oh, thank God! I thought I'd gone deaf."

My wife tells me that whenever I say, "Yes Dear," she knows that I'm not really listening. That's because *hearing* is passive, while *listening* is active. When we truly listen, we use not only our ears, but our eyes, our intellects, and our emotions.

Most salespeople are thought of as talkers, not listeners. People might say, "She really has the gift of gab" or "He's just a born salesperson. Although speaking is important, listening is even more important in sales success. Yet the National Society of Sales Training Executives did a study that showed that salespeople's biggest shortcoming was that they didn't listen. Take the quiz in Exhibit 2.1 to assess your listening skills.

Exhibit 2.1
Your Listening Quiz

As you answer each of the following questions, rate yourself from one to five on how you listen:

Never ←――――――――――→ Always
1　　　2　　　3　　　4　　　5
(1=never, 2=seldom, 3=sometimes, 4=usually, 5=always)

1 2 3 4 5　　1. Do you enjoy listening to other people?

1 2 3 4 5　　2. Do you encourage other people to talk?

1 2 3 4 5　　3. Do you listen, even when you don't like the speaker?

1 2 3 4 5　　4. Does the speaker's gender affect how you listen?

1 2 3 4 5   5. Does the speaker's age affect how you listen?

1 2 3 4 5   6. Does the speaker's background affect how you listen?

1 2 3 4 5   7. Do you listen to friends and strangers with the same intensity?

1 2 3 4 5   8. Do you maintain eye contact with the other person?

1 2 3 4 5   9. Do you use appropriate facial expressions to show interest?

1 2 3 4 5   10. Do you use appropriate body language to show interest?

1 2 3 4 5   11. Can you concentrate entirely on what the other person is saying, instead of mentally rehearsing what you are going to say when he or she stops talking?

1 2 3 4 5   12. Are you successful at blocking any distractions that might take your attention from the other person?

1 2 3 4 5   13. Are you generally aware of any unspoken messages?

1 2 3 4 5   14. Are you generally aware of "pacing," matching the speaker's mood, energy level, and body language?

1 2 3 4 5   15. Do you let people finish what they're saying?

1 2 3 4 5   16. If they hesitate, do you encourage them to go on?

1 2 3 4 5   17. Do you restate what others have said and ask if you got it right?

1 2 3 4 5   18. Do you withhold judgment about ideas until the other person has finished talking?

1 2 3 4 5   19. Do you listen, regardless of the manner of speaking and the choice of words?

1 2 3 4 5   20. Do you listen, even though you are sure you know what the other person is going to say?

Add up your points. If you scored more than 85, you are a very good listener. If you scored between 95 and a perfect 100, you're entitled to skim the rest of this chapter and go on to Step 3! (I have to admit that, although I specialize in sales communications and work very hard at my listening skills, even I don't have a perfect score.)

LISTENING PAYS BIG BENEFITS

We live in a talking society. We are bombarded by TV and radio talk shows. Everyone in authority—priests, ministers, rabbis, teachers, experts, and almost all managers— offer us wise words and instructions. Everywhere we're surrounded by talk, talk, talk, but it's the rare person who is an active and accomplished listener. To really connect with our customers, we need to stop talking and start listening.

Listening is a much underrated skill, but it pays good money. Psychiatrists, psychologists, and therapists all charge a substantial fee just to listen. Sympathetic bartenders and hairdressers are rewarded with generous tips. Good salespeople are also well paid, usually in direct proportion to how well they listen. (Australian communications trainer Doug Malloff says, "The only ones willing to listen to your problems for free are your dog at feeding time and a good salesperson.")

Customers spend their money where they believe they are getting full value, and part of that value is feeling important. If you listen to them, make them feel important, prove you have their best interests at heart and are eager to meet and exceed their expectations, then you can keep those customers forever.

LISTENING BUILDS TRUST

Listening is the best way that I know of to build trust because it shows that you are truly interested in the speaker. Let them tell their story. Don't interrupt with solutions. Let them finish their statements. Most problems between people can be defined in one common phrase: "You never listen to me." When customers say that, they phrase it a little differently. To themselves they say, "You're not listening to me." To you, they just say, "Goodbye." The difference between *united* and *untied* is where you put the "i." Listen in a way that keeps you united with your customers. Make them the center of attention, and keep the "i" where it belongs.

Recently a salesperson came to our office selling wholesale frozen meat, chicken, and fish. Each item was packed 12 to a box and appeared to be of excellent quality. The price was attractively low. My wife, who is also my business partner, told him she wasn't interested in his product if she had to purchase a dozen of each item. She wanted to know if she could mix a box so we would have four each of the meat, chicken, and fish. He answered that the beef was range fed and the fish was flash frozen on the boat while still at sea to protect freshness. My wife said she understood that the product was of good quality, but could he sell us four of each item, making a dozen total. He answered that if we thought the price was too high, he might be able to give us an additional 10 percent discount if we bought three boxes—a dozen of each item. My wife explained once more that there were only two of us, and we didn't want three dozen. He answered that the product would keep in a freezer up to six months.

At that point she realized that he was not listening to what she was saying. They were not communicating. She was not responding to what he was saying, and he certainly was not responding to what she was saying. The interview was over.

LISTENING CONTROLS THE INTERVIEW

Exceptional communicators have learned that a listener controls the results of a sales interview. Salespeople who don't listen don't sell. They also don't learn: "You ain't learnin' nothin' when yer talkin.'" And they lose a powerful way to prove that they are interested in the customer. When we listen, we gain insight into our customers' feelings and beliefs. We build trust, understanding, and credibility while clarifying misconceptions. But we only accomplish these things with *active* listening. Passive hearing doesn't do it.

DOING WHAT COMES UNNATURALLY

Studies show that average adults spend about 80 percent of their waking hours in some form of communication. If you were to keep a record of your day, how many hours do you think you would spend talking and how many listening? I'll bet, if you are successful in sales, 60 percent or more of your active time is spent listening. The other 40 percent is divided between speaking, writing, and reading. Usually, the more listening, the more sales.

The good news is that listening can be learned. There is no such thing as a born listener. The best selling tip I can give you is: *Learn to listen*. "Nature has given us one tongue but two ears, that we may hear from others twice as much as we speak." Euripides said that in ancient Greece, and it still holds true today.

COPING WITH DISTRACTIONS

There was an emergency once when I was at a seminar in a large hotel. A lady rushed to the microphone and cried, "If you can't hear what I'm saying, go quickly and tell a security guard!" Of course, if you couldn't hear what she was saying, you wouldn't know to inform a security guard. Probably everybody was able to hear her, but many stopped listening in the ensuing panic.

Listening is never the same as hearing. Hearing uses only the ears. It's a physical process that goes on all the time. We can't close our ears like we can close our eyes. Our ears are noticing sounds, even while we sleep. Hearing is the last of the five senses that works as we fall asleep and the first that works when we wake up. That's why alarm clocks ring.

We face a constant cacophony of sounds: birds chirping; refrigerators, copy machines, and air conditioners humming; radios blaring; background music playing in stores and elevators; children shouting; dogs barking; cars honking; clocks ticking; flags flapping; and the wind soughing and moaning through the trees. As a defense against aural overload, we've learned to turn off the path from ear to brain. We don't notice at least half the sounds around us because we have stopped listening.

Listening is hard work. Most of us are too lazy to work that hard. We want to be entertained and informed without a lot of effort. Once we recognize this weakness in ourselves, we gain a powerful understanding of our potential customers and their own communication processes. Our customers are not trained to listen to us— in fact, just the opposite. They are often trained *not* to listen to us. When they hear anything resembling a sales pitch, they automatically turn off.

Much in life is just background noise for our own thoughts. Very little on radio or television requires serious listening. In fact my wife says I drive her crazy when I've got the remote control in my hand. I can watch three television programs at once and tell you what's happening in all of them.

Our prehistoric ancestors knew that the faintest sound could signal terrible danger or potential dinner. Today, with no hungry predators and plentiful supermarkets, we can afford to ignore most noises. And because the sounds around us can demand so little of us, we've trained our minds to wander. A key phrase can send us off on a private train of thoughts richer and more fulfilling than the words going on outside our heads. We tune out and turn our attention inward. However, effective sales communicators consciously deny themselves this luxury. They focus entirely on the words of the customer, even listening with a "third" ear to extract feelings and contradictions.

HAVE YOU BEEN LISTENING?

Here's a little test for you. Be honest. What else have you thought about while you were reading the last three pages? Why? You're supposed to be reading and listening in your mind. But the truth is that the average reading speed is about 200 words a minute, while most intelligent people think at somewhere between 800 or 1,200 words a minute. Since reading is really just creating sequences and images in your mind, you have generated four of your own words for every one of mine. So, unless my information is extremely important to your immediate welfare, you are probably going to think of other things as well.

This is even more true when someone is talking to you. When a customer says "I really need delivery on Thursday," a nonlistening salesperson might respond, "Okay, but let me tell you the other features of this product." If that salesperson had really been listening, he or she would have realized that the sale was already closed.

What can keep you from listening to your customer? A lot is in your own head: all your knowledge, experience, and judgment. But you also come fully equipped with opinions and prejudices. As you react to what you are hearing, any of these factors can get in the way and block understanding.

Other barriers include words and phrases to which you respond negatively. There are topics that you may not be comfortable discussing. There are regional accents, inappropriate language, slang, even profanity, that may cause you to judge the speaker, thereby derailing your listening skills.

Sometimes your preconceived ideas or biases get between you and communication. Sometimes you are rushing or facing a deadline, and you don't take the time to listen. Sometimes you are anxious or overloaded, and you just don't want to be influenced.

Anything that closes your mind is your enemy. Good listeners keep their minds open. Your job is to listen with absolute openness and flexibility, no matter what the background and characteristics of the speaker. Focus on what the speaker really wants to communicate rather than what you want to hear. This may require increased concentration. It's very easy for your own thoughts and fleeting impressions to take control of the communication process, but don't let them. Suspend your personal thoughts and feelings and just listen. This means putting yourself in someone else's shoes, so to speak. When you listen actively, you will nearly always see your customer's point of view.

THE WORLD'S MOST FASCINATING CREATURE

We invariably listen to what interests us. As salespeople, we can make a conscious decision that the most important, fascinating, beguiling, enchanting, dazzling objects in the entire universe are our customers and potential customers—even when they don't offer us an immediate benefit. Then, no matter what the distraction, we will hear the smallest thing.

There's an old story about a man who dropped a coin on the plush carpet of a crowded hotel lobby at a banker's convention. Everyone stopped and turned. When something is important to you, you have the ability to switch from hearing to listening. Hearing is automatic and passive, done with our ears, a physical response to sounds. Listening is an active choice, done with the brain, a learned response. We choose to listen, to pay attention, to take in the sounds that matter to us. One of the best salespeople who every worked with me was a fellow named Keith Sheffield. Keith had a very simple but powerful listening philosophy. He said, "The customer is the most important thing in my life right now. Nothing will distract me from him, his interests, and his problems." Keith was an amazing salesperson because of that principle. He looked everyone in the eye and listened intently to what his customers said. If he was sitting in a chair, he would lean forward slightly. If he was standing, he stood tall in an attentive stance. His prospects thought he was the most interesting person in the world because he was interested in them. They believed this because of the eagerness with which he listened. Prove to your customers that they are important enough to capture your full attention. Be enthusiastic in gathering the information you need in order to respond intelligently to your customer's needs. If the customer says, "What I really need are fewer break-downs—we lose so much time," an active listener will respond, "Can you tell me what kind of breakdowns you're having and what you're doing to handle them?" You, the listener, are giving feedback that shows you are focused on the customer's interests. As these interests are revealed, you can tailor your responses. If you do that con-sistently, in most situations you will find that the customer will also meet your needs.

Nod your head. Say:
- I understand.
- I see.
- Can you tell me more about that?
- Can you give me an example?

This provides you with more information, indicates your attention, and invites your customer to agree, correct you, continue, or elaborate.

THE MOST PRECIOUS MOMENT

Sound is fleeting. When someone is talking, you either get the message right now or it's gone forever. You rarely have more than one chance, so pay attention. Dr. Richard Weaver II, coauthor of *Listen to Win*, says that real listen-ing is a three-step process: Hearing, thinking, and feeling. "This means you must involve the physical, the mental, and the emotional."

Force yourself to focus on the speaker's intent. In other words, listen actively. Concentrate not only on what a word means but what happens when it is used. Pay attention to the words, the tone of voice, and the pictures the speaker is transmitting. Listen actively for ideas, feelings, the main point, the truth, and for consequences.

People make many decisions based on information they didn't actually hear. We read between the lines or hear between the words. That's when we're really listening. We observe body language, facial expressions, eye contact, visual impressions, posture, and gestures.

LISTENING TO IMAGES

Actor David Niven was in the hospital, dangerously ill and awaiting surgery. A group of his friends rushed to the hospital only to be told that he wasn't allowed visitors. They gathered outside the open door of his room and peered in. Niven weakly raised his hand with his thumb up. Did he communicate? Yes, and they were all listening—but with their eyes.

Baseball legend Yogi Berra once said, "You can observe an awful lot by just watching." Good sales communicators know that's true. You have to use your ears, your eyes, your intellect, and your feelings to be a real listener. When we use all of our senses, we can hear what is said, what is not said, and what is really meant.

Getting Customers to Listen

With so much aural confusion going on around us all the time, how can we encourage our customers to listen to us and not the dozens of other things happening in the immediate vicinity? By using the following techniques:

- **Asking questions.** To answer questions, customers have to listen, maybe even ask you to repeat the question. You've engaged their attention.

- **Confirming understanding.** Use questions like, "Do you see any advantages in faster delivery?" This forces customers to consider whether faster delivery is an important motivation. You've engaged their intellect.

- **Observing and pacing body language.** Whether customers respond or resist, this provides valuable clues to attitudes and motivations. You've engaged their feelings.

- **Not interrupting.** Sometimes a pause, even a long pause, doesn't mean that your customers are through expressing an idea. Conquer the impulse to jump in with your own brilliant ideas before you've learned the whole story.

When you ask questions, check for understanding, respond to body language, and wait patiently and expectantly for your customers to finish, you require them to focus on their exchange with you. Everything else becomes background noise.

LISTEN AS IF YOU'RE DEAF

Tony Parinello, a fantastic sales trainer, radio host, and author of *Selling to Very Important Top Officers*, tells how he learned the importance of listening intently. In his book, he tells how losing his hearing actually improved his sales because he taught himself to read lips. It forced him to concentrate on the customer with his eyes glued to their lips and his mind focused.

> *Back when I was selling large computer systems, I had a number of very important sales meetings with the president of a good-sized company. I was always right out on the edge of my chair, watching him like a hawk. I'd get as close as I could without violating his personal space. If there was a distraction—if a secre-tary walked into the office, for instance—I wouldn't let it divert my attention. I couldn't afford to miss a single word of what the president had to say.*

Tony sold this company a large computer system. With the commission, he treated himself to two powerful, nearly invisible hearing aids. His first sales call after getting these hearing aids was on this same customer.

> *It was great! I could hear everything! I didn't have to lean forward in my chair anymore! I asked the president, "How's the installation going?" And as he started to tell me, guess what happened? I didn't have to look at his lips anymore! Why, I could look around the room! When there was a noise, I could turn to see what it was. When the secretary walked in, I could smile and nod hello.*

> *All of a sudden, the president stopped right in the middle of his sentence. I turned and looked at him. He looked me right in the eye and said, "Tony, take your hearing aids out. I feel you're not listening to me. I felt really special before you had those hearing aids. You used to watch every move I made. Please take them out. And I did.*

That moment Tony recognized one of the most important truths in his sales career: When you're with your customers, listen to them as if you're hard of hearing! Listen to them as though you must read their lips. Give them your undivided attention.

FOUR TYPES OF VERBAL INTERACTION

Dr. Lyman K. Steil is famous for his listening seminars. (He is the president of Communication Development, Inc. and former chairman of the Speech Communication Division in the Department of Rhetoric at the University of Minnesota.) He told me that he believes in the "Minimum 51 Percent Rule:" We must accept no less than 51 percent of the responsibility for successful communication no matter if we are the sender or receiver. That means that you, the successful salesperson, control the selling situation by listening for meanings as well as words.

"Words," he says, "have no meaning. *People* have meaning." Supplying that meaning is an internal process. We create meaning from our experiences, knowledge, and attitudes.

Dr. Steil notes that there are four distinct types of verbal interaction:

- **Phatic communication.** This is what sales communicators call rapport building and includes small talk, the conversational gambits that build relationships.
- **Cathartic communication.** This is cleansing conversation where we unload feelings, ideas, or anger. In selling, this is called probing for motivations.
- **Informational communication.** This is used for both qualifying and probing, giving or getting facts and feelings to the other person.
- **Persuasive communication.** This is used during the presentation and for closing the sale, or to reinforce or change existing attitudes, opinions, feelings, beliefs, or actions.

Two Types of Listening

Listening is an important connecting skill, but this doesn't mean that you must focus totally on every single word your customers say. Such obvious intensity could make them uncomfortable. Effective listening has a variety of levels. When you listen to your customers, your concentration level will vary from casual to total, depending on the internal rhythms of the interaction. In *Effective Listening: Key to Your Success,* Dr. Lyman Steil divides listening into two types: social and serious.

TYPE #1: SOCIAL LISTENING

Social listening is the first step to connecting, and it has four categories.

1. **Appreciative listening** takes place when we hear a poem, concert, or TV program that interests us, that gives us satisfaction and pleasure.

   There's a music store in my neighborhood that I love to go to. You're never sure what kind of music will be playing when you walk in, but it's always stimulating. The salesman's voice is so fascinating and melodious that I could listen to him forever. He knows his product and he has an uncanny ability to sell me music that speaks to my soul. Even though I have a huge record, tape, and CD collection, it is such a pleasure to do business with him I keep making up excuses to go back and buy more.

   You won't use appreciative listening as a connecting tool, but remind yourself that your customers will. Keep your voice pleasant and your attitude supportive and friendly. Make it a treat to listen to you.

2. **Conversational listening** is a two-way give and take. We listen attentively and then we speak and hope the other person is listening attentively also.

   Frank Snowden is a manufacturer's rep selling bicycles and bike accessories. He has been calling on the same stores for a number of years. Frank thinks of himself as a partner in their businesses; almost a co-owner. With that attitude and because he has been calling on the same stores for so many years, Frank arrives and starts chatting with his customers about what's going on in the business, what the competition is doing, and what other stores are using for promotions. At the same time, he's restocking their shelves and setting up displays. Frank's style is so personal and so conversational, you'd never know that he was selling anything, and yet he is one of the top producers for his company.

Conversation is the social glue that connects people: "What do you think of this weather?" "Have you lived here long?" "I love that too!" Never dismiss conversation as irrelevant to the sales process, but never let it replace solid questioning and interaction. Get to the point, or you'll find yourself back on the street with warm feelings and little else.

3. **Courteous listening** is often one-way listening. What's being said may not be especially relevant to the listeners, but they nod, smile, or frown as appropriate and offer occasional brief comments. This may be the way you listen to a gabby neighbor or an eccentric shopper behind you in the checkout line. When you find yourself in situations where there seems to be no benefit in continuing the exchange, you will nonetheless listen *courteously* because you never know! Some casual exchanges can end in enormous paybacks. At the worst, you allow others to feel good about themselves and to think you're an intelligent person.

4. Respectful listening is listening to a superior. It is a child listening to a parent, an employee listening to an employer, a younger person listening to an older person, a student listening to a teacher, and, hopefully, a salesperson listening to a customer. Even though you are presenting yourself as an expert, listen respectfully. Remember the anecdote about the woman who dined with two famous British statesmen: "When I talked with Gladstone, I was convinced he was the most fascinating man in the world. And when I talked with Disraeli, I was convinced that I was the most fascinating woman in the world." Obviously Gladstone spoke brilliantly, but Disraeli *listened* brilliantly.

Good salespeople treat customers as if they are the boss, because they *are*. The owner of the service station where I buy all my gas always tries to wait on me personally. He asks how my car is running and he listens attentively. One day I thanked him for making me feel so important. He said, "Of course. You *are* important. You're a steady customer. I try to be friendly, listen, and give good service to all my customers, but especially the steady ones. You're the ones who pay my mortgage, send my kids to college, and let me live the good life."

TYPE #2: SERIOUS LISTENING

Serious listening is the kind of listening you'll usually do when you're with a customer. According to Dr. Steil, serious listening can be either *selective* or *concentrated*.

1. Selective listening is when we listen only to part of what's being said. Usually this means that we have already decided what kind of information will be important to us, and we're waiting for it to come along. Everything else we ignore. In some situations this is very useful, like waiting for your name to be called in the doctor's office. But in the sales process it can be disastrous. If you prejudge what you hope to hear and then wait for the customer to say it, you can miss the most important points.

2. Concentrated listening is when we focus on everything the speaker says. This kind of focus can take enormous energy, but it is essential in a selling situation. Be ready to shift to high-powered concentrated listening at a moment's notice.

THE **HEAR** METHOD

A good current book on listening is *Listen to Win* by Curt Bechler, Ph.D., and Richard L. Weaver II, Ph.D. When I talked to Dick Weaver, he explained some of the major listening traps. When we receive a piece of information, we tend to twist it around so it coincides with what we think is being said. We filter and adjust the information to meet our own personal expectations. The filters we use are our egos and our past experiences. Dick says that effective listening is actually a process of reduction. First, we perceive through our senses. Then we make assessments and apply the information. Finally, we perform an action or have a reaction.

Dick suggests using the HEAR method:

Hear the message.

Engage in summarizing.

Ask questions.

React appropriately.

These four steps provide feedback, clarification, and encouragement to the speaker.

LISTEN WITH YOUR EYES

Remember what your mother used to say: "Look at me when I'm talking to you." She was really trying to teach you to be a super salesperson. Can you imagine anything more disconcerting or insulting than to be talking with someone whose eyes constantly shift to look at something else in the room?

A saleswoman I knew, Ginny Morvay, taught me the value of good eye contact. She used it one day to get a good table in a crowded restaurant. Her secret was to make the maitre d' look her right in the eye. Most of the time this isn't what happens. The maitre d' is looking down at his reservation list or across the room to spot a table. Ginny wouldn't say a word to the maitre d' until he made eye contact. She had learned in her selling career that when you get people to look you in the eye, they treat you as a person, not an object. Ginny told me that when she could keep eye contact with a potential buyer, she almost always made the sale.

RESPECT THE COMFORT ZONE

Another consideration for good communication is personal space. Most of us have territory that we consider our own. This varies according to culture, custom, age, sex, and inclination. We don't want other people pushing into these areas unless we give them permission. For most people, the distance between speaker and listener is very important. Too far, and you seem aloof and cold. Too close, and you seem intrusive or threatening.

Northern Europeans, for example, prefer a greater average talking distance than people do in countries farther south. A joke in diplomatic circles is that, at a party for English and Arab officials, after a half hour or so, all the English will have their backs flat against the walls facing a circle of approaching Arabs. The English keep moving back to open up the space. The Arabs keep moving forward to close the space.

Sexual differences can also play a part in personal space. In a fascinating study, it was shown that males of all ages tend to talk most freely when standing or sitting side by side. They feel slightly threatened by someone standing directly in front of them. This could be interpreted as confrontational. Females, on the other hand, are slightly uncomfortable talking to a stranger who stands beside them so they can't make eye contact. They prefer face-to-face, eye-to-eye communication.

Another study found that people imprisoned for violent crimes had a much larger discomfort zone than the average noncriminal. Some felt personally threatened, even violated, by someone standing 10 feet behind them—a possible explanation for their apparently unmotivated attacks.

When you invade other people's space, they stop listening to you and start self-talking, an internal conversation about who you are and what your intentions are. The salesman I mentioned earlier, Keith Sheffield, was very effective at closing sales by leaning slightly toward the speaker and listening intently. Obviously he had an excellent sense of receptiveness because this approach could cause some customers extreme discomfort. As a good sales communicator, you must learn to judge the comfort zone between you and the other person.

Dr. Edward Hall, author of *The Silent Language*, feels that people have four distinct distance zones when they are communicating.

1. **Intimate distance** includes holding a child, caressing a spouse, or hugging a friend. When others violate this space, such as on a crowded train or elevator, we react by ignoring the person, pretending he or she isn't there. In more threatening situations, we may confront the person or flee. We certainly don't listen.

2. **Personal distance** is the normal distance in a sales situation, a casual conversation, or small group gatherings. In this space, we are close enough to be heard and to see the other person's physical reactions; maybe even close enough to touch, such as when we shake hands. Still, if we get too close, the other person will back away and put up a temporary barrier, making good sales communication more difficult.

3. **Social distance** is more prevalent when the other person is a stranger, when we are suspicious, or when we have a reason to create a

separation. If a salesperson seems aggressive, the listener may well step back or even maneuver an object, such as a desk, between them as a form of protection.

4. **Public distance** is usually found in large public gatherings or when a speaker is talking to an audience. This space creates few opportunities for a meaningful exchange of dialogue.

THE PEN AND PAD TECHNIQUE

Good salespeople are usually good note takers, whether on paper or in their heads. I recommend paper. This shows the customer that you are really listening, and it also provides a record of what was said. Remember the old saying, "The palest ink is stronger than the strongest memory." Take notes that are clear, brief, and cover all key ideas.

PRESCRIPTION FOR DIFFICULT CUSTOMERS: LISTEN!

You've seen signs posted in stores saying things like, "If you break it, you buy it," "We reserve the right to refuse service to anyone," or "Shoplifters will be prosecuted to the full extent of the law." All these are one-way communications, and most of the time the customer pays no attention to them. How do you react when you have a customer who says, "Just give me the facts quickly. I'm in a hurry," or "Let me tell you what's wrong with your product," or, even better, "Sit down and listen, son, I'm gonna tell you how to run your business." Then there's the rare customer who believes all salespeople are crooks: "I may need your product, but I'm not going to believe anything you tell me. I am not going to let you sell it to me." Are these also one-way communications, or can you turn them into dialogues by *listening*? There are all types of prospects, but remember that everyone wants to be approved of, understood, and made to feel important. No matter what prospects say, effective sales communicators listen for the meaning behind the words, then respond to these needs.

LISTENING TO BAD NEWS

From time to time we must all give and get unpleasant news. Since no one likes to hear bad news, listeners may not register the information at first. They may have to hear it repeatedly and even require some time to absorb it. There's an acronym for the sequence of listening responses to unwanted information: SARA.

Shock and disbelief

Anger, both at the news and the messenger

Rejection and denial

Acceptance of the inevitable

People may pass through these stages in a few seconds or minutes. In cases of extreme loss, the stages may take weeks or months.

Top salespeople have learned to soften the blow by being superior listeners. Using questions and feedback, the skilled salesperson can help customers through the first three stages to acceptance, as in the following example:

Mr. Jones, I know you're going to be really disappointed that we can't extend credit to you right now. Especially since you've been in business so long at the same location, and your reputation is excellent. You might even be angry and want to do business with someone else. But, this is just the beginning of our relationship. We have the product you need at the best possible price, and we guarantee delivery this week. Our only problem is that this is the beginning of our sales relationship, so we need cash payment for the first order. As soon as this formality is over, we'll extend you credit on your next order.

This example recognizes all of the stages of SARA that our customer is going through.

Feelings are as important as facts, sometimes more so, and we can't deny the natural reactions when we hear unpleasant news. But remember the maturity gap. We have an emotional reaction to almost everything we hear. Maturity is recognizing valid emotions and responding intellectually. The shorter the time between emotional reaction and intellectual response is an important measure of our maturity. When we are dealing with conflicts, we must almost always deal with emotions first.

If a customer is upset and not moving to an intellectual level as quickly as you would like, be patient. Help this person along. Give feedback. Show understanding and be empathetic.

What if you find yourself getting angry or distressed in response? What an angry customer wants, more than anything else, is to be listened to, but it is hard to listen effectively when the customer is yelling or being sarcastic. Still, that is when we must be most attentive. This is the most important moment *not* to fake attention, tune out, interrupt, or let emotion of the moment block out the customer's real message. Listen for both facts and feelings.

If you find listening to this customer at this time is more stressful than you can tolerate, try to back off. Give yourself time to calm down. Excuse yourself. You might say, "Please excuse me ...

> ... while I go check some information in the file."
> ... while I get another opinion."
> ... while I clarify the company's policy."

Use any explanation to get yourself some time to calm down, but be sure the customer believes you are truly listening and trying to help him or her.

Once you get yourself under control, ask the customer, "What would make you happy?" Listen to the answer. If the customer wants something that is totally unreasonable, use a version of the Feel-Felt-Found technique:

> *I know how you* feel. *I've* felt *the same way in a similar situation. And I wanted action. Please tell me again how we can both win in this situation. How can we solve this problem and find a solution?*

This shows that you're listening. Try to find some area of agreement to build on. Prove you take your customers and their problems seriously. Use all of your listening skills to show they are truly important to you.

Everyone has types of information that push emotional buttons. We all respond to certain stimuli, and when we respond emotionally, our communication skills are diminished. Advertising people are paid high salaries to create words and pictures that reach us on an emotional level. Teachers, politicians, religious leaders, and the media are all skillful at appealing to our emotions. As conveyors of emotionally charged information, salespeople need to recognize when they themselves have become emotional. Identify what can push your own emotional buttons and make you lose control, then rehearse dealing with your feelings. We all need to practice putting our feelings in perspective and controlling our emotional responses.

10 Listening Do's

It's possible to listen yourself into a sale. Just follow the 10 commandments of listening.

1. **Recognize the importance of listening,** particularly in sales. Salespeople who don't listen don't sell. Those who can't close their mouths never close the sale.

   I once had a salesman work with me who demonstrated the product better than anyone I had ever seen, but he was one of my most ineffectual salespeople. He started his demonstration at point A and went straight through to point Z. He didn't let anyone interrupt him. As a result, he talked right past the sale. Many salespeople talk themselves out of a sale. I've never heard of a salesperson who listened himself or herself out of a sale. Be sure you are aware of your need to listen.

2. **Concentrate on the message.** Larry Frank, who is with ComDoc Office Systems, says that listening helps create a partnership with the customer, which is the most successful way to sell. According to Larry, asking questions, listening intently, and talking only when you have something to say is the secret of building that partnership and the secret of sales success.

3. **Listen for main ideas.** In every conversation there is a tremendous amount of extraneous speech, but somewhere in that gobbledygook there is a main thought, a main idea. Good sales communicators try to identify that primary concept.

    Bill Stack, of GE Information Services, says that he tries to learn the strategic plan and long-term goals of his customers. Whenever his customers refer to that idea, Bill's feedback tells them that he is listening and may have a program that is appropriate for achieving their goals.

4. **Listen for the real meaning behind the words.** We rarely say all we mean. Sometimes we don't want to bore people. Sometimes we're intimidated. Sometimes we fear showing our deep emotions. To make a sale, listen for the opinions and feelings that are not expressed.

    One of my friends, John Gray, has what I think is the toughest selling job in the world. He is a funeral director, and his real business is to sell funeral services, caskets, preparation of the deceased, and transportation services to and from churches and cemeteries. John is the best listener I've ever met. He's always dealing with people who are in emotional turmoil. They are extremely vulnerable and would be easy to manipulate. But John, like most funeral directors, listens while he comforts. From the conversation, he is able to extract their desires for their loved ones, discover their financial capabilities, and then match his product to their emotional and financial needs.

5. **Don't be judgmental.** Give your speaker the benefit of the doubt. Look beyond the statement to the intention.

Years ago when I was in the investment business, I had an experience with multiple distractions that almost stopped me from making the biggest sale of my life. It was my birthday. My great-uncle was in the hospital after a heart attack, and I was busily trying to complete the paperwork on my desk so I could take the remainder of the day off. Suddenly my office door opened, and there stood a very large man in not-very-clean bib overalls. He stared sharply at me and said, "I come here to git the free book about makin' money." His manner and his words did not encourage me to believe he was going to be a large investor. My mood was, "How can I get rid of this person so I can get out of here?"

Luckily, something triggered my realization that this was a prospect who deserved my attention as much as any other prospect. I invited the man to sit down and tell me about the investments he had made in the past and what his desires were for the future. I was quite surprised when the first words out of his mouth were, "My wife just inherited more than a million dollars, and we don't know nothin' 'bout that kind of money."

6. **Listen to other people's points of view.** Empathize. Try to understand where they're coming from. Dean Rusk, former Secretary of State, said, "The best way to persuade others is with your ears."

In 1965, I worked with a salesman named John Shaw. John was a great guy, but not a great salesperson. Month after month his sales totals were among the lowest of the 14-member sales team. Our sales manager had tried everything to encourage John, but couldn't seem to motivate him. But suddenly one June, John sold more than any other salesperson in the organization, almost half again as much as his nearest competitor. What had happened? The sales manager had really listened to what John wanted.

On a visit to John's home, his manager noted the family's closeness and also that they had no color TV, a major purchase in those days. The manager casually asked John's wife and children if they had thought about getting a color television. Their response was very enthusiastic. Then the manager announced that the bonus for the top salesman for June would be the largest color TV on the market.

He had listened empathetically and "heard" that John really wanted a TV to please his family. He listened for motivations and found a way to encourage John in a unique and personal way.

7. Use questions skillfully. If you don't understand something or feel that you've missed a point, clear it up right away before going on. Give feedback to check that you're on target. Use questions such as the following to confirm that you understand:

- Bob, how much money do you think this benefit would save you?
- In what ways would this plan be better than your old one, John?
- So, if I heard you correctly, Mrs. Stone, you would use this service to improve delivery time?

Use phrases like "Let's see if I'm clear about this. You're saying that … " or "Then you feel your situation is … " When you give feedback, both you and your customer know that you're on the same wavelength. And, because you are identifying with your customers' needs and wants, you will be better able to serve them.

8. Relate the relevance of what you're hearing to your objective. Most salespeople would say, "Well, my objective is to make a sale." I hope you'll expand that to say, "My objective is to make a sale, to serve my clients' needs and wants, and to solve their problems." Is what you're hearing enabling you to offer solutions that will accomplish this?

9. Resist distractions. External distractions include background noise or a customer with faulty speech or a physical flaw. Internal distractions can be poor concentration, time constraints, or physical needs. Fight to prevent these distractions from interfering with your active listening.

Janet Hayden, a travel agent in San Francisco, is adept at staying open to clients despite lots of distractions. The travel agency business can be hectic. Phones are ringing, faxes are clicking, and everyone is in a hurry. But you would never know that Janet had another customer or another concern except you. I asked her how she handled it. "It's simple," she said. "I listen to my clients. I really hear what they are saying, and I'm not satisfied until I can discover what they want and repeat it in terms that make sense to them. I never try to shorten the selling cycle. I listen with an open mind. I answer their questions, and, eventually, I work out a travel plan that is just right for each customer."

10. **Give feedback.** Let customers know they're getting through to you. Say things like, "I understand that point," "Maybe you would repeat this point for me," or "Is what you're saying ... ?" Be sure that your feedback is honest, not platitudes you use because you're not paying attention. Your customer will know the difference.

ANALYZING SUCCESS AND FAILURE

Think about your most successful listening experience. Why was it successful? Was it due to your skills as a listener or to the speaker's ability to transmit information in a way that was acceptable to you?

What about a listening experience you had that was a total failure? Your objective was not met, nothing was achieved, and there was no sale. Why did that happen? Did you have empathy and rapport with the speaker? Did you understand what he or she was saying and check to be sure? Did you process the information in the way it was being presented—auditorially, visually, or kinesthetically? Did you identify the speaker's motives and decide if these motives were in harmony with your objectives?

Isn't it interesting that when we are checking on ourselves, we usually pay more attention to our intentions than to our actions, but when we are checking others, we always pay more attention to what they do and rarely look deeper into their intentions.

THE YELLOW BRICK ROAD TO SUCCESS

I once heard a speaker tell the story of *The Wizard of Oz*, but with a different twist. He talked about how Dorothy had just one objective: to get home to Kansas. That's all she talked about. She didn't give mixed signals. She had a single purpose, a single goal, a single destination. She voiced her objective often to everyone who would listen. But there were other characters in the story, too. The Scarecrow wanted a brain and he talked about it. The Cowardly Lion wanted courage. The Tin Man wanted a heart. Each had a single objective, and, because each voiced their own objective and listened to the others', they were willing to cooperate so all of them could reach their goals and achieve their desires. Keep that story in mind when you're selling. Good communication means that you listen to the other person's objective and state your objective so you can form a bond, or partnership, between you and the customer and anyone else involved in the transaction. In that way, you can all reach your personal goals. That means win-win selling and win-win communications.

STEP THREE

ASK QUESTIONS (DO I UNDERSTAND WHAT YOU'RE SAYING?)

A door-to-door salesman asked a little girl playing on a front porch if her mother was at home.

"Yes," she said. He rang the bell and knocked for several minutes, but no one answered.

"I thought you said your mother was home," he said.

The child replied. "She is. But I live next door."

Moral: Questions are the oldest and best method of sales communication, but only if you ask the right ones.

I n ancient Greece, Socrates was asked, "How are you doing?" "Compared to what?" he responded. Socrates was noted for answering questions with questions.

Salespeople do that, too. One customer asked, "Why do you answer a question with a question?" The salesperson replied, "Why not? Can you suggest a better way? How would you do it?" Asking questions is the salesperson's power tool. You can't spend too much time learning to ask. When you ask, you get. The more you ask, the more you get. The Bible says, "Ask and you shall receive."

Most salespeople have taken that advice to heart, but not all of them know how to go about it. In a recent study conducted by The Sales Development Institute in Upper Darby, Pennsylvania, 87 percent of the 300 salespeople surveyed said they understood the value of asking questions, but only 27 percent demonstrated an ability to ask a well-thought-out, stimulating series of questions.

Selling isn't telling. Selling is asking. Questions prospect for and qualify potential customers, check comfort boundaries, establish needs and desires, define interest, and tell us when we can close a sale.

BENEFITS OF QUESTIONS

Questions accomplish more than any other technique in a successful sales communication. They help you to listen actively, direct the conversation, and get feedback. They help establish rapport. They help you move on to the next stage of the sales process. They help to monitor the listener's acceptance, understanding, and interest.

Questions are a great hook. They focus on the most important part of the sales communication at that moment. People are forced to give their attention when they are asked an intelligent question. They must listen, they must think, and they must respond. That is why it is important to be sure that you are asking the right questions.

Questions and answers create an environment for agreement. They build trust. They increase buying desire by building empathy between you and the customer. You show a real interest in the customer when you ask questions like:

- What do you think you need to get the job done?
- What do you feel is your biggest problem?
- I understand how the company feels, but what is your personal opinion?

The following questions also help to discover customers' feelings and opinions so you can determine their primary needs, wants, and motivations:

- If you could have anything, what would you want my product to do for you?
- What kind of employee turnover do you have?
- What does it cost when you train a new employee who quits soon afterward?
- Is computer downtime a problem for you?

As they answer, your customers usually realize there is a need to be filled. Ask customers how they are trying to solve a problem and how they feel about the results they are getting. Ask them how continuing to do what they have been doing will produce different results. Focus their attention on alternatives: "How well has that worked for you?" "Are you satisfied with those results?" "What would better results mean to you?" If they don't see a problem, you can't possibly sell features, benefits, and motivations to solve it.

Questions are among the best tools in your selling kit. Handled well, they bring out the prospect's needs, desires, and prejudices. The inexperienced salesperson tells and shows and tells and shows until prospects become disinterested or even antagonistic. Skillful questioning, on the other hand, draws prospects out and leads them to decide to buy. When prospects feel they've made that decision themselves, they "invest" in it. They are more convinced of its soundness and are prepared to defend it. Your proposal, which prospects might have been inclined to challenge, has now become their own idea.

Why People Don't Buy

In all my years of selling, I have found only six reasons why people do not buy:

1. They don't know what you're selling.
2. They don't need what you're selling.
3. They don't want what you're selling.
4. They don't have the authority to buy what you're selling.
5. They can't afford what you're selling, even with good financial terms.
6. They don't believe in you and your product.

When potential customers truly don't have the money or the authority to buy, no question can overcome that problem. If they truly don't need your product, you would do a disservice by creating an artificial need. In these cases, no matter how good your questioning skills, sometimes the sale just can't be made.

OVERCOMING DISTRUST AND DISLIKE

But you *can* question your way to a sale if the problem is lack of desire or confidence. Here are some examples:

- How can we make you happier?
- Maybe you could tell me what you think?
- What would be the first thing to do now?
- How would you suggest we handle this?
- Are there any points we haven't covered?
- What is the next step we should take?
- What process should we follow to move us along?

Ask, or call for action, or make a request, such as:

- Can you decide today?
- When will you be ready to make your decision to consider this product?
- How can I get you to give me the order?

Questions like these allow you to take control of a selling situation and change your customer's perceptions.

COULD YOU HELP ME?

Don't be embarrassed about asking for favors. I believe no one can succeed in selling if they don't learn how to ask. Don't let your ego get in the way. One of the most effective sales questions is still, "Could you help me?" For example:

- Could you help me get a clearer picture of your problem by showing me how that works?
- Could you help me by explaining your customers' short-term business and personal objectives? Do you have a list of those?

- Could you help me by recommending one of your friends who could also use my services?

It's an intriguing irony that people tend to feel kinder toward people who owe them something than toward people they owe. They prefer the company of their debtors to their creditors.

SUDDENLY THEY GET IT

People tend to do what they are asked to do. In my seminars I often ask, "Can somebody lend me a pen?" And someone always does. Then I add, "And will someone give me a watch?" And they do. "Can anyone give me a five-dollar bill?" And a dozen people in the room reach into their wallets to pull out their money. I collect these items and place them on a table at the front of the room. Then I go on with my seminar, completely ignoring them. It takes less than a minute for everybody in the room to catch on. "Yes," I admit, "I asked and I received."

People are trained from childhood to do what they are asked to do. When your mother asked you to clean your room, you cleaned your room. When the teacher asked you to do your homework on time, you attempted to do it. When Dad asked you to help him cut the lawn, you helped. It's a habit for most civilized people. So, if your customers are asked, they will react. It makes them feel important when you ask them to do something. It brings them into the selling situation, which is an essential step toward making the sale.

Asking is the fuel that drives the engine of sales. Your sales slow down when you stop asking the right questions, but when you become an expert at asking, there is no speed limit.

THE PRICE OF ASKING

There is a price when you ask for help and get it. You must show appreciation. You must show gratitude. You must show cooperation. There is a strong inference that you now owe the givers something, and that you will repay this debt by having their best interests at heart. You can never lose by asking, as long as you're willing to honor this commitment and pay this price.

THE SEVEN CATEGORIES OF QUESTIONS

Since you first asked "Why?" as a child, you've been using questions, but you probably weren't aware that they fall into seven distinctive categories.

1. Open-ended
2. Reflective
3. Directive
4. Multiple choice
5. Closed-end
6. Throwback
7. Confirming

Each type has specific strengths and weaknesses, advantages and disadvantages, in the selling process.

1. Open-ended questions can't be answered with a yes or no response. Their strength is that they solicit information about emotions and thoughts, facts and feelings. Open-ended questions are used to probe and gather information. You design them to find out what is really on your prospect's mind while you introduce your own ideas. The open-ended question relies on the six classic questions of journalism: who, what, when, and where (primary probes), plus why and how (used as secondary probes for follow-up questions).

The primary probes are used to gather information and facts. Some open-ended probing questions are:

- What is your opinion about … ?
- What do you feel the real problem is?
- When do you see this happening?
- Where could you install the new equipment?

Open-ended secondary probes are particularly valuable for discovering feelings and motivations. You can ask:

- Why did you say that?
- How do you feel about … ?
- Why is that important to you?

Use open-ended questions to determine both facts and feelings.

2. Reflective questions rephrase previous statements or questions into another question. Reflective questions give prospects a chance to rethink, review, or restate the facts and ideas that led to their previous answer. These questions help you determine objections or problems by firmly fixing customers' reactions in their own minds. Some reflective questions are:

- Then you feel your situation is (repeat what the prospect has said).
- So, Joan, you said you think this method would (repeat what the prospect has said).
- As of now, your experience has shown that …
- Let's see if I'm clear about this. You're saying that …

- Well, you've already tried something like this, Mary. Do you feel that … ?

Reflective questions help you to clarify and define areas of concern that your customer may not be aware of or has not been able to express clearly. When using reflective questions, keep genuine concern in your tone of voice and any judgmental tone out. People don't care how much you know until they know how much you care. Demonstrate your concern with the tone you use in asking these reflective questions.

3. Directive questions direct and focus prospects on decisions you want them to make. These questions are often used in "trial closings"—questions that show whether the prospect is ready to close. Your directive question expands a given idea or given point, clarifies the prospect's thoughts, or helps him or her decide if the benefits are desirable.

The words "would," "could," and "should" are helpful in directive questions. A good communication technique is to pause and look thoughtful before asking a directive question, then say something like:

- In what way would this plan be better than your old one?
- I assume you agree that this service could bring benefits that you're not receiving now?
- Would you tell me more about this situation?
- How much money or time do you think this benefit would save you?

4. Multiple choice questions offer choices and are usually a form of the directive-question technique. We make choices every day. That's what a free market economy is all about. But those choices can be directed by skillful sales communication. When you offer customers an option, you can direct their attention to the decisions that will make up the sale. For example:

- Would you like delivery on Tuesday or Wednesday?
- Red or black?
- Cash or charge?
- Regular size or large economy size?
- Would you like to buy one more and get the 15 percent discount?
- Would you like tinted glass, wire wheels, stereo or radio, leather seats, sun roof, or stick shift?

Any time you offer choices, you have an opportunity to direct your customer toward the next step in the sales process. Multiple-choice directive questions are invaluable, but be sure you don't overdo it.

Recently I walked into a coffee shop, hungry for breakfast. The waiter asked, "What would you like this morning?" I said, "Eggs, bacon, potatoes, and coffee." The waiter asked, "How would you like your eggs: fried, scrambled, or soft boiled? Do you want your bacon crisp or extra crisp? Would you like the potatoes plain or with onions and peppers? Would you like toast with that? White, wheat, rye, raisin, or English muffin? What kind of jam or jelly would you like—grape, strawberry, or marmalade? Would you like regular or decaffeinated coffee? Black or with cream?" I was exhausted by the time he had finished taking the order.

5.   **Closed-end questions** require a yes or no answer or a very short, factual answer. Examples include:

- Do you rent or own?
- Do you usually finance your purchases?

- During what hours does your shipping department accept deliveries?

Closed-end questions are useful for narrowing down options. When you ask a closed-end question, you may be expecting a favorable response. However, if the customer says no, your interview could be over. Inexperienced salespeople often back themselves into corners with closed-end questions.

Question: *Do you understand what I mean?*
Answer: *Nope.*

If you get that answer, you have to start all over again.

Question: *Is this product the one you'd like to buy?*
Answer: *Nope.*

You've just lost the sale. You need to become an expert at asking closed-end questions. Frame them so they either keep the exchange going or close the sale. Try asking the following questions:

- Can you think of any reason why this wouldn't work for you?
    If your prospects say no, they've agreed it will work for them, and you've closed the sale. If they say yes and offer an objection, you've simply got another objection to overcome. Some more good closed-end questions are:
- Have we covered all your concerns?
- Have I shown you how this is going to pay for itself in six months?
- Do you know of any other product or service that can beat ours?

All of these questions either close the sale or give you an opportunity to continue. Design your closed-end questions so that when the prospect says no, it means yes.

There's a wonderful George Burns and Gracie Allen radio show from 1947. Gracie is a pushover for door-to-door salespeople, so George makes her promise to "just say no" to any question they may ask. So the doorbell rings, Gracie answers, and there's a salesman.

Salesman:	*Good day, madam. Do you have a piano?*
Gracie:	*No.*
Salesman:	*Would a piano be too expensive for you?*
Gracie:	*No.*
Salesman:	*Do you think your husband would object if you bought one?*
Gracie:	*No.*
Salesman:	*Would just one piano be enough?*
Gracie:	*No.*
Salesman:	*I'll put you down for two. Will tomorrow be soon enough for delivery?*
Gracie:	*No.*
Salesman:	*This afternoon then. Would you like easy credit terms?*
Gracie:	*No.*
Salesman:	*That'll be COD, two pianos at $10,000, delivered this afternoon. Thank you very much, ma'am.*

This radio routine was funny because it tapped into one of the fears customers face. They are afraid they may be tricked into an answer they do not intend to give. Good sales communicators never try to trick their customers. They know a short-term gain may mean a long-term loss.

Good sales communicators use closed-end questions to solicit simple facts or to bring the sales interview to a decision point. Closed-end questions can be dangerous, so use them sparingly or when you feel certain the prospect is ready to make a decision.

6.   Throwback questions question the question. Whenever possible, you can retain control of any situation by answering each question with another question. This forces your customers to continue to clarify their own thinking. Of course, you'll answer their questions, but, whenever possible, answer with another question. Here's an example:

Question: *Is this the best price you can give us?*
Answer: *Is 10 percent above wholesale low enough?*
Question: *Could we wait until next week?*
Answer: *Do you want to make an appointment for then?*
Question: *Is this really unbreakable?*
Answer: *What if we agree to replace it free if it ever breaks?*

To answer your question, prospects must think through their position and explain or defend it. Whenever possible, let prospects provide the reason why the information you're giving is meaningful. You supply the facts and figures, but piggyback them on throwback questions.

- We have several payment plans. Would you like to go over them now?
- The total price is $998 per unit, plus $25 installation fee. Would you like us to install them, or do you want to handle that yourself?

Years ago I worked with a sales master named Ernie Gonzales, who answered every question with a question.

If someone asked, "Can you give me a discount?" Ernie answered, "Would 10 cents off the price help you make a favorable decision? Would you prefer a small discount or a service guarantee?" No matter what the prospect asked, Ernie had a "question answer."

Ernie encouraged prospects to defend their positions. Most people are suspicious of sales talk, so if you can learn to get them to say what you would have said, it is much more powerful. People believe what they themselves have said and defend these beliefs.

When customers take a position, they usually defend it. So, if you use questions to help them reach a decision and put it into words, it is theirs and they are committed to defending it.

7. **Confirming questions** are what I like to call "Irish questions." We Irish are famous, or perhaps infamous, for ending every statement with a question mark. "It's a nice day, isn't it?" "You're an American, aren't you?" "It looks like rain, don't you think?" There's a great story about an Irish actor who had only one line in a play: "It is." He went around rehearsing that line over and over again, trying dozens of inflections. On opening night, he walked up to the leading lady and said, "Isn't it?"

Professional sales communicators know they can get their customers' attention and confirmation just by adding a question at the end of each statement. For example:

- This service will save you time, don't you agree?
- Your secretary could use this, couldn't she?
- You see the benefit of this, don't you?
- This product will solve that problem, won't it?
- This would look great in your office, wouldn't it?

If customers disagree, then you have your second most valuable asset—an objection. They'll tell you why they don't agree, and this allows you to address their concerns. On the other hand, if they do agree, you have a confirmation, a point that is acceptable to your customers. When you get enough confirmations, you can assume the sale. It's an excellent practice to confirm each point along the way.

I was teaching this technique at one of my seminars, and a salesperson came up to me during the break and said, "I'm not very good at getting confirmations, am I?" But he was, wasn't he? He asked a question at the end of his statement and that's how you get a confirmation, isn't it?

One of the best examples of using the confirming question happened years ago. I was training some real estate people to sell resort condominiums on a golf course. One of the salespeople, Ed Nash, had a routine that he never varied. After showing models, he would drive the people around the golf course. Near the ninth tee there was a small hill, and from there you could look out over the golf course and beyond to a beautiful valley of orchards. Ed would always stop his cart at that point and say, "This is the most beautiful view in all of California, isn't it?" It was a rare prospect that didn't agree. Then Ed would ask the question that I insisted every salesperson ask: "Can you think of any reason why you wouldn't want to look at that view every day?" Almost every customer would respond, "No." That question and answer often made the sale.

DON'T OVERDO IT

Regardless of what kind of questions you're asking, ask just one question at a time. Listeners are easily confused, so don't make it worse with multiple-part questions. It's okay to have multiple choices but not multiple parts.

This was one of the hardest lessons I ever had to learn. My wife tells me that I used to come home at the end of a busy day and say, "Honey, do you feel like cooking or would you rather go out to dinner? And if we go out to dinner, would you like Italian, Chinese, or just plain American? And if you do want Italian, by the way, would you like to go to the place downtown or the place over by the freeway? And after dinner, what about a show, or would you rather come home and watch TV, or perhaps just read?" She swears I never took a breath between all of these questions, and there is no way she could possibly give me a meaningful answer.

Never bombard customers so they don't know which question to answer first. Never ask a new question before the first one is answered. If you have a list of questions, present them one at a time. Pose the question and then keep absolutely quiet so you can hear the entire answer. I call this the "Golden Silence." Only when a look or gesture clearly indicates that the ball is back in your court should you go to the next question on your list.

Ask, but never demand. Pressure always creates tension. To get cooperation, ask pleasantly, and expectantly. Asking nicely is always the best way to get what you want.

In my seminars, I demonstrate this with a simple exercise. I walk up to someone in the audience and say brusquely, "Put out your hand." I put the palm of my hand against theirs and push. Almost always, the person resists and pushes back. We can get into a real struggle in a very short time.

Then I walk over to someone else, put out my hand, and say, "It's really nice to meet you. May I shake your hand?" This person always takes my hand.

When you apply pressure, most people struggle and rebel. But when you ask politely while showing your care and concern, the response is almost always favorable. Don't confront, ask aggressively, demand, or insist. Don't cross-examine your prospects or put them on the defensive. Ask politely.

In fact, ask permission to ask. In my book, *Questions That Make the Sale*, I quote John Hammond, president of the American Motivation Association, which organizes sales seminars. He thinks that asking permission to ask is one of the most important steps in information gathering. He said, "Mr. Bethel, we've been able to help thousands of people at companies just like yours. We may be able to help you. But to determine that, may I ask you a few questions? Would that be all right?" John says that if you don't ask and get permission, you risk two situations. Either prospects may be reluctant to answer your questions because they're not sure why you're asking and what's in it for them, or else you may find yourself hesitating to ask the questions that you need to ask.

QUESTIONS AND THE SALES PROCESS

There's a joke about two people who run into each other and have been talking for several minutes when one says, "Hey, you haven't asked me yet how business is."

"So, how's business?"

"Don't ask!"

In this case, "don't ask" is a colloquialism for "not good." We could almost turn that around and say that "ask" can be a synonym for "good," or at least for "effective."

When I had an office in the financial district of San Francisco, I was often approached for a handout by a neat, middle-aged man in faded work clothes. He wasn't the usual panhandler. He was clean, neatly dressed, pleasant, and articulate. He politely asked everyone who passed, "Could you help me out with a little change?" Most people didn't stop, but a few did.

Month after month, he stood there, and month after month my curiosity grew. Finally I stopped and asked him if I could buy five dollars of his time to ask him about his work. He agreed, for indeed he thought of what he was doing as a selling job. He told me he worked five days a week, five hours a day, from 8:00 a.m. to 9:30 a.m., for an hour at midday, and from 4:00 p.m. to 6:00 p.m. The most profitable time was lunch time. About one passerby in twenty gave him money, usually 25 or 50 cents, though every tenth "customer" gave him a dollar. His total earnings averaged $40,000 a year, tax free. He was very happy with his job. "Where else could I make this kind of money with no skills and no training, working just 30 hours a week?" And why did people give him money? Because he asked them to!

Questions are a great tool at every step of the sales process. Whether we are prospecting, probing for information, defining problems, or seeking solutions, the technique of asking moves us ever closer to a sale. Let's explore how to use questions throughout the sales process.

PROSPECTING QUESTIONS

Prospecting is the first and most important step in the sales process. Every sale starts with prospecting, even when you're dealing with old customers who have purchased from you many times. Old customers may have new needs. Do more checking, ask more questions, and open yourself to new opportunities. Some prospecting questions could be:

- May I talk to the owner?
- Who is your toughest competitor?
- Can I use your name if I call next door?
- Is there someone else you think this service could really help?
- Would you introduce me to someone who could use my services?
- Have you found any new uses for our products?
- Do you know of anyone else who could use our product in this new way?

PROBING QUESTIONS

Probing means discovering your customers' needs and wants. With effective probing, skilled communicators move themselves to an advisory position where they become partners with their customers, conferring on something of mutual importance. Successful probers gather information about the person, the business, or the project. Some effective probing questions include:

- Could you tell me what your duties and job responsibilities are on a daily basis?
- How exactly do you define your target market?
- Which is most important to your company—engineering, production, finance, or sales?

Probing questions are usually open-ended. Many are nondirective, sometimes called the "soft probe." Probing helps you discover your potential customer's needs and wants. You use probing questions throughout the entire selling process, but especially before you go into your presentation. Begin by asking:

- How long have you been using the equipment you have?
- Which model is your favorite?
- And does that work well for you?

For the last 25 years I have watched Jerry Sexton sell new homes in subdivisions. He is a master of the probing technique. Prospects must pass through the sales office on their way to and from the model homes. When they arrive, Jerry's communication goes something like this:

Jerry:	Hi. I bet you've come out here today to see our models, haven't you?
Buyer:	Yes, we were just driving by and thought we'd take a look.
Jerry:	Great. Let me get you a map of the layout and a list of the features and benefits so you'll know what you're seeing as you walk through the models. By the way, do you own your own home now?
Buyer:	No, we're renting.
Jerry:	There's nothing wrong with renting, except that you don't build any equity and you don't take advantage of the appreciation of real estate. You'd like to get in on that, wouldn't you?
Buyer:	We've thought about it, but quite frankly we don't know if we can afford the down payment.
Jerry:	Do you and your wife both work?

Buyer:	*No my wife is expecting our second child, so she had to leave her job. But she'll be going back three or four months after the baby's born.*
Jerry:	*How old is your first child?*
Buyer:	*He's four.*
Jerry:	*He'll need a room of his own, then, won't he?*
Buyer:	*Well, if we could afford it.*
Jerry:	*I guess the only problem today is to see if you like our models and figure out how you can afford one of them, right?*
Buyer:	*I guess so. Do we go through here to look at the models?*
Jerry:	*You sure do. And on your way back, let me tell you how you really can afford this house. In fact, you can't afford to pass it up.*
Buyer:	*Okay.*

When you ask probing questions, customers must stop whatever they're thinking about to focus on your question and their answer to it. Most people can't think of other things while they're answering a question.

Probing questions follow what I call the 3-D format:

1. Define
2. Develop
3. Decide

Your questions lead prospects to *define* their needs, *develop* solutions, and *decide* how to implement them.

Defining probes: You ask about the current situation and the prospects' needs and problems. You point out problems or needs you may have observed or you suspect might be true because of your experience with other customers. Never tell customers what their problems are. Ask until they tell *you* what their problems are.

Defining probes also help you and your customer agree on which problems should be addressed. You could ask:

- What is your major concern right now?
- Which is more important to you at this time?
- When you say your budget is limited, what do you mean?
- What results do you hope for?
- What results do you expect?
- What have you done in the past that was successful?
- What have you done that didn't work?

These are all defining probes. They gather information that defines your customers' needs, wants, and expectations.

Developing probes: You ask about decision-making criteria, stimulating and bringing into focus the ideas, opinions, and concepts that might lead to an acceptable solution. Examples include:

- Will you decide this yourself or do you have to get approval from your boss?
- Is there a committee or a team that looks over our suggestions?
- What is the lowest failure rate that you have been able to hope for?
- How often do shipping problems hold up your assembly process?
- Could you think of a better way to deal with that?
- Which is more important to you right now, gross revenue or bottom-line profits?

- Do you feel that customer satisfaction increases profits?
- What would represent success to you?
- Can you think of a better way to deal with this problem?

You, the salesperson, must create questions that help the customer identify and consider both problems and solutions regarding price, quality, delivery time, value, reliability of service, and any other criteria that are important to him or her in the sales process. Your development probe should ask the client for possible solutions. Through questioning you can lead the prospect to admit that your product or service fulfills most of the criteria that are important to them. You can ask if there's any reason why your product or service shouldn't be selected to fill their needs.

Deciding probes: All of the following questions ask the customer to decide how to proceed. They move you along to the next step in the sales process.

- So, do we agree that your first job is to outline everyone's duties and responsibilities, and then to work out an implementation schedule?
- What payment arrangement would work best for you?
- Will a dozen of these be enough for an initial order?
- If I agree to have half the units delivered by the first of the month and the rest within two weeks, will you authorize the purchase order today?
- May I see you on Thursday at 4:00 p.m.?
- How do you feel about trying the plan I've just recommended?

Practice deciding-probe questions until you master them. Lead your prospects to define their needs, assess their problems, identify solutions, and determine how to implement them. That is sales communication at its highest level.

Personalized probing. Let's review some of the results that you should expect when you use the probing technique. Your first probing question should capture attention, position you favorably in the customer's mind, establish a personal rapport, and open the door to more questions. That's a tall order, isn't it? But remember the importance of first impressions. Don't ask a poor question that will get you into trouble in the first five seconds.

Probing questions can help you spot dissatisfaction or show you how you can do something better. If you hit the right question and get customers honestly sharing their opinions and feelings with you, you have a better chance of making the sale. You get them involved with personal questions. I don't mean, "How's your golf game?" or "How's your son doing at Harvard?" In today's busy world, your first questions should be business oriented. But you can still personalize the questions, focusing on the duties, responsibilities, and actions of your listener. Tie your questions to their business interests. Try asking:

- What's your competition doing?
- The last time we talked, you were trying out a new procedure. How's that working for you?
- What's your company's market share on that particular product?

Inexperienced salespeople often start out with, "Well, how's business today?" What if business is lousy? And "How are you doing today?" What if the customer's personal life is a disaster? In good sales communication, your questions should always lead your customers to the answers you want. Sometimes your customers aren't even aware of their own feelings and beliefs about some part of their business. Your questions can uncover information that your prospects aren't even aware of yet.

PROBLEM QUESTIONS

Sometimes customers don't know they have problems. But if you, the salesperson, can uncover a problem that you can solve, you are potentially performing a useful service, and so deserve to make the sale. Experienced salespeople develop a repertory of effective problem questions that can reveal potential difficulties and dissatisfactions. If no problem or need exists, no sale is made.

After your initial probing questions, your next questions should determine the present situation and establish prospects' thinking about needs and wants. These are problem questions. For example, you could ask:

- Did last year's storms catch you unprepared?
- Does your staff duplicate work because your computers aren't networked?
- Is there any problem at all that your customers could have when they use your product?

Your customer may think everything is great, but your job is to determine the true situation and see if there is a problem. If your customer is already aware that something is wrong, your questions will bring that out in the open and help you understand the problem.

Recently I watched Rick, a salesperson at the Video Only store in San Mateo, California, turn a casual browser into the purchaser of a 27-inch television set. As Rick approached, the browser said he was "just looking, not buying today." Rick began some skillful questioning that went like this:

Rick:	*How many TVs do you have?*
Browser:	*Just one.*
Rick:	*How old is it?*
Browser:	*About eight years old. It still works fine, but it's small.*
Rick:	*Since your set is eight years old, maybe you'd like to see some of the new technology that is available today?*
Browser:	*Okay, I guess so.*

At this point, Rick took the browser to a large chart on the wall that listed all the features of the latest sets. He explained each feature, relating it to a potential benefit.

Rick:	*How does your old set measure up to these new features?*
Browser:	*Well, like I said, it's got a small screen. It doesn't have that picture insert feature, and it certainly doesn't have the surround sound. The sets you've shown me are an improvement.*
Rick:	*Which of these new benefits would you use the most?*
Browser:	*I think that picture insert feature is interesting, but just having a big new set with a clear picture in the living room is something the whole family would like.*
Rick:	*So you've decided it would be a good idea to have a new set?*
Browser:	*Yes.*
Rick:	*What's keeping us from doing business today?*
Browser:	*Money.*

Rick: *Let's go over to the counter and see if we can work out a payment program that fits your budget. Maybe we could delay the first payment for three or four months and still deliver the set tonight. That would be a good idea, wouldn't it?*

At this point Rick walked the browser to the counter and began to figure out the financial details. He had turned a browser into a customer. This is an example of defining customers' needs and wants, developing interest and desire, and asking questions that allow customers to decide on a solution.

However, if you try to offer solutions before you've clarified the problem and the need in your prospects' minds, you will fail. You need to let them discover their own needs and decide on the solutions. Play the role of supporter and advisor. Show that you care about the outcome, not just making the sale. Ask questions like:

- Forget about my product. What do you feel you need to get the job done properly?
- Are you still more concerned with growth than with income on your investments?
- Is the immediate cost the most important factor in your decision, or are you more concerned with the long-term value?
- If you could change anything at all in your schedule or your operations, what would it be?

Tony Alessandra, Ph.D., and Phil Wexler, authors of *Non-Manipulative Selling,* put it this way: "People buy services and products most often because they feel that they and their problems are understood by the seller. They don't buy because an insistent salesperson makes them understand the product." What kind of doctor do you want to go to? The one who examines you for 15 seconds, hands you a prescription, and departs, or the one who listens to all your symptoms and fears, explains alternative treatments, and then designs a special program of medication, diet, or exercise based on your input? Which treatment would you be most likely to follow? Which doctor would you go back to if the first prescription didn't work?

Inexperienced salespeople usually think they can spot the problem and the solution before the customer has finished describing it. *Don't*. Force yourself to continue ending your sentences with question marks. And when you're absolutely certain what the problem is, ask even more questions to confirm that the client also sees the problem.

Never try to solve the problem for the customer. Describe possible solutions and then let the customer solve the problem with your consultive help.

OVERCOMING OBJECTIONS

What are the prospect's objections? Find out at the same time that you overcome them by using questions.

Prospect:	*We just replaced all the equipment in this department a year ago. It took my staff nine months to learn how to use the system. I'm not going to go through all that trouble and expense again just to save a few returns.*
Salesperson:	*About how many returns are you getting?*
Prospect:	*A few, but not enough to make new equipment worthwhile.*

At this point the salesperson can explore whether the returns really are a problem. Here are some possible questions. (Remember not to ask them all at once! Stop and listen to each answer before framing the next question.)

Salesperson: *You say a few returns. How do you handle them? Do you give straight refunds on returns or do you ship replacements to your customers? Who receives the returns? Who checks out the defective parts to confirm the problem? Who ships the replacement? Who handles the paperwork? Does any of this ever cause you any overtime? How does your bookkeeping department handle the exchange? How long does it take them? Do you ever have a problem carrying over outstanding credits for returns? Do you ever offer clients a discount or offer free replacements to keep them happy? Do you personally follow up with clients who return defective parts? How often do you have to do that? Do you supervise the people responsible for handling the returns? How much time does this take? Have you ever had a client threaten legal action because a part malfunctioned? Do returns affect your insurance rates?*

The prospect is probably starting to have a different idea of what defective parts are costing the company. But what if the prospect is still reluctant because of past problems:

Prospect: *Yes, I agree there's a problem, but it took my staff nine months to learn how to use their new system. I'm not going to go through all that trouble again.*

Salesperson: *What made your new system so hard to learn? You say it's complicated; can you give me some examples? Do you think your staff had a special reason for resisting the change? What kind of instruction did your people get? Did you have professional training? Was it done in-house or in outside classes? Was it done by the company that sold you the equipment? Are the same employees still with your company? What effect has the new equipment had on your turnover?*

Here are some more objection-countering questions:

- Is this equipment too sophisticated for your available workforce?
- Does this price seem like a lot of money to you? Should we stop for a few minutes and figure the actual costs so we can see how much money these features can save you?
- You say your current system is good enough. Would you recommend it to other companies? Are there any tips you would give them about potential problems? (Listen for the problems!)

With questions like these, you overcome objections. Even more important, you make prospects recognize problems at the same time you make yourself their ally in solving them.

COMMUNICATING VALUE

Is the problem big enough to justify the solution? When customers perceive that their problem is more expensive than the cost of solving it with your product or service, you've probably made a sale. If, however, the problem is small and the cost of the solution is high, it is unlikely a sale will result. One of my acquaintances, whom I'll call Ralph, sells computers. Recently he called on an office where the employees were still using typewriters. He almost couldn't believe it.

Ralph:	*Doesn't typing things over take an awful lot of your secretaries' time?*
Prospect:	*Yeah, I guess it does.*
Ralph:	*If you bought my computer with a word-processing program, you could eliminate retyping. In fact, you could enter form letters and reproduce them by just touching one key.*
Prospect:	*What's the cost?*
Ralph:	*You can buy the entire computer with the monitor, keyboard, built-in word-processing program, and, of course, a laser printer for about $8,000 or $9,000. How does that sound?*
Prospect:	*It sounds like a lot more than I'm paying my secretary. I only write about six letters a week. Most of her time is spent just filling up the boxes attaching shipping labels, which she writes by hand. I guess your gadget could save her some time, but it would cost me a lot of money.*

In this scenario, the customer simply didn't see the value of Ralph's product, so no sale was made. When you explore the problem, find out more about it, identify the customer's difficulties and dissatisfactions, and ask how your product and service can help, you establish value in the customer's mind. If customers believe the cost is too high, they won't buy.

FOUR STEPS TO ESTABLISHING VALUE

Value is the balance between the cost of a problem and the cost of a solution. You can establish value with questions. Questions can uncover needs, highlight problems, and encourage customers to offer their own solutions.

Before you contact the prospective customer:

1. **Make a list of problems** you are aware of for this particular customer at this particular moment.

   My stepson, Mike Murray, recently heard about a charitable organization that was given 200 computers. The company that manufactured the computers had come out with a faster and better model, so they decided to rid themselves of their factory inventory by making their stock available to a charity and taking an income tax deduction. Now, what was the charity going to do with 200 computers? Michael made two lists. The first listed all of the problems a charitable organization would have marketing 200 computers without conflicting with the donor company's distributors, customers, and future prospects. The second listed solutions, identifying organizations and government agencies in the U.S. and in foreign countries that could not afford to buy computers at the current market prices.

   Michael then contacted the charitable organization and showed them how they could perform good work by selling the computers at a much reduced price in domestic and foreign markets. After all, isn't that what the charity wanted? To make some income while they were helping others who were in need? Michael acted as broker and made a small commission. Everyone was happy. Everybody won.

2. **Plan questions** that will focus the customer's attention on the value of solving these problems. Show the affect of these problems on

some aspect of his or her business: cost, time, energy, productivity, morale, or profits.

3. **Ask the prospect why** it is important to solve the problem. What does he or she think would help, and how can you, through your products and services, make his or her life easier? For example:

Salesperson: *I've estimated, from what you've said, that returns are costing you about $25,000 and about 200 hours annually. How would your life be different if you got your return rate close to zero, if you personally saved about four hours a week, and if you could do both of those things for less than it is now costing you?*

4. **Ask for more advice than you give.** Let the customer write the dialogue, proving the value of the product to you, by asking questions like these:

- How would you advise other people about this model?
- Would you recommend this? Why? Why not?
- How have you used this? What are its best features?
- Is this big enough for your needs?
- Is this what you had in mind?
- How else could this save you money?
- If I could arrange a free trial, how do you think you'd use it? What would you try to accomplish?

You can actually learn new things about your service or product while customers write their own sales pitch.

CLOSING QUESTIONS

When you're ready to close the sale, you don't want any surprises. The questions you've used throughout the sales process can lead you to a natural closing:

- Can you think of any reason why this isn't the best solution for you? No? Then how would you like delivery?
- What is our next step?
- Who else should I talk to before your company decides?
- Shall I check the delivery schedule on that?
- Do you need to get a purchase order or is your signature sufficient?
- Will three be enough for the time being?

Rarely should you say, "Will you buy?" Instead, use other questions to confirm that the prospect is willing to buy. A close is not just asking a buying question at the end of a presentation. It's the entire sales process, from precontact planning to closed-end questions.

Closing the sale has been compared to buttoning the last button of an overcoat. As your customer accepts each benefit, one more button is being buttoned. As you confirm your customer's needs, wants, desires, fears, and prejudices, you lead him or her to discover his or her own motivations and how your features and benefits will make his or her life better. Finally, when you get to the last button, you close the sale. Here are some buttoning-process questions:

- What do we need to do to get this done?
- What kind of support service would you want from us?
- Shall I check the delivery schedule on that?
- How does that sound to you?
- Can you think of another solution that would work better for you?
- Shall I put a hold on these for you?
- Would you prefer to schedule the support training before or after the installation?
- Check or charge?
- UPS or U.S. mail?
- What else can I do to make sure you're happy with this purchase?

Questions like these either get the order or take the sales process to its next logical step.

WHICH QUESTIONS WORK?

Knowing which questions to use and when to use them is the key to your sales success. Start keeping a record of what works for you. Use a computer file, a card file, or a notebook. Keep track of the questions that worked and those that didn't.

Philosopher and mathematician Bertrand Russell once said, "I don't know who you are. I don't know your company. I don't know your company's product. I don't know what your company stands for. I don't know your company's customers. I don't know your company's record. I don't know your company's reputation. Now, what was it that you wanted to sell me?" Your questions must identify your customer's problems and your right to offer solutions.

STEP FOUR

Speak Clearly
(How do you say it?)

A young woman asked her boyfriend if she had the most beautiful eyes he'd ever seen.

"Yes," he said.

"And the most beautiful smile?" "

"Yes," he replied. "

And the most beautiful hair?"

Again he said, "Yes."

"Oh, John," she cried, "you say the most beautiful things!"

How you present an idea is sometimes as important as the idea itself. Saying the right words at the right time in the right way can make or break a sale.

What is the most compelling point of your sales presentation? Your job is to know all about your product and to show how it will make your customers' lives better. You even have a responsibility for making sure the product is used appropriately and doesn't make your customers' lives worse.

Master salespeople communicate all the basics and much more to their customers. No matter how sophisticated prospective buyers are, they are rarely as sophisticated at communicating or as knowledgeable about a product as the person who is selling it.

Master salespeople are wordsmiths. Isn't wordsmith a nice term? It implies that you have developed the power to forge and mold language by stringing together words, phrases, and concepts that will influence behavior. When we use language in its original and most immediate state, we call that speaking.

Here are some interesting facts about speaking. Did you know there are about 3,700 languages and dialects in this world, and, counting technical terms, English speakers can draw on more than a million words? But the average college graduate recognizes only about 30,000 words and uses just 5,000 of them in everyday speech. But even 5,000 words provide a rich and lively selection to draw on to ensure that you can always say what you mean.

How would you rate yourself as a wordsmith? How would you rate your speaking skills? Do you speak up? Do you use the appropriate volume? What about your pacing? Do you use pauses effectively? Do you vary the tone of your speech? What about the pitch of your voice? Does your voice reflect eagerness, concern, cheerfulness, gravity, respect, sincerity, or dignity as appropriate to the situation?

SPEAKING CORRECTLY

When you really want to be heard do you speak loudly or softly? Research has shown that soft speech is accepted more readily. I don't mean quiet speech, and I don't mean so soft that your listener can barely hear you. I mean soft tones. The easiest way to achieve this is to think kind thoughts about your listener. But that's not enough. When you're nervous, under stress, or have poor breathing habits and posture, your customer may interpret the way you're talking as hard or harsh.

Good sales communicators project a professional, interested, expressive voice. In fact, when you become conscious of the tone of your voice, you will be able to use it as a barometer of your own stress level. Intriguingly, you can then use this awareness as a self-regulating tool, actually relieving stress by consciously adopting a calm, modulated tone of voice.

Your voice is the vehicle that transports your words to your listeners. The tone of your voice can influence them almost as much as your words. Work on creating a positive tonal quality, a voice that expresses alertness, confidence, and interest. Keep a smile in your voice. A smile is contagious. You build a positive image for yourself and your company when your voice conveys that you are a pleasant, kind, happy person.

Expressive voices express. Would you rather listen to a well-modulated voice or one that is flat, tired, nasal, or grating? Strive for a natural, normal tone of voice. Talk at a moderate rate. Vary your pitch and timbre, emphasizing meaning through the color and vitality of your voice. Be sure to articulate: "What's happening," instead of "Whasapanin"

Tape record your voice and listen to it. Would you enjoy listening to it for hours at a time? If not, what needs to be different? Listen to others. Do they have a positive effect on you? If they do, what are they doing to create that positive effect? How can you apply that to your voice, words, and phrases?

START WITH STRESS RELIEVERS

Speaking involves tightening lots of muscles and clenching your mouth to force air through your vocal cords and over your tongue and lips. Add to this your anxiety about communicating effectively, and speaking can be hard, tense work. Learn to relax. The following techniques will help you improve the tone of your voice:

1. **Yawn.** I bet you did when you read that. However, it's impolite to yawn when you're talking to a customer, so practice when you're alone. Feel what happens inside your throat. Your vocal cords seem to open up.

2. **Relax your jaw.** A tight jaw makes your voice sound tight. Pretend that your jaw, chin, and neck are made of gelatin. Flexibility produces softer tones.

3. **Breathe.** You particularly need good breathing techniques when you're going to speak

softly. Try this exercise. Inhale through your mouth and let the air extend your lower torso below the navel. Your chest should hardly move. You should feel as if the air is going to the very bottom of your body. Try five deep breaths right now. Put your hand on your chest to see if it moves. As you exhale slowly, imagine that your muscles are all falling toward your spine. This helps in developing softer tones.

4. **Pant.** How softly can you pant? How loudly can you pant? Pant as long as you can, then take a deep breath and pant again. Repeat with "Oh, Oh, Oh, Oh" and then "Ah, Ah, Ah, Ah." Practicing these breathing exercises will help you build a strong voice and enable you to use the soft, controlled tones your customers will appreciate.

5. **Stand up straight.** Relax your neck and throat, open your mouth, and slowly repeat over and over again, "ding, dong, ping, pong, king, kong." Don't be afraid to move your lips, tongue, and jaw. Start high and each time you say the phrase, say it in a lower and lower register. This will help you pull the words down into your throat where the sound is deep and has resonance. If you repeat this exercise several times a day you'll lower and improve the tone of your voice.

Learn to play your voice like an instrument. Put emotion into it. You prove your interest in what you're presenting to your customer when your voice comes alive and shows enthusiasm. Remember that your voice is painting a picture. What does it look like?

YOUR SELLING VOCABULARY

You already know all the words you need to motivate people; the skill is in choosing the right ones. But that doesn't mean you don't need to strengthen your word power. The larger your vocabulary and the better your understanding of language, the more successful you will be at communicating. Good sales communicators develop a sales vocabulary, constantly finding new, emotionally charged ways to say the same things about their product.

Some years ago I was helping a company build their sales team. One of the salespeople I hired was Al Wisgardi. Every day Al would practice explaining the product with words that he had never used before. Very difficult. Al's self-imposed vocabulary challenge became something of a joke to the other salespeople.

But Al soon had at least a dozen ways to describe the product without repeating himself. This gave him so many different ways to reach and motivate the customer that he rarely missed a sale. It had started as a game, but soon every salesperson in the company was emulating Al. They carried their dictionaries in their briefcases and spent spare moments looking up words and trying to figure out how to fit those words into their presentations.

USE EMOTIONALLY CHARGED WORDS

Words appeal to emotions in positive and negative ways. There are three main categories of emotional words: expressive, dynamic, and personal.

Expressive words. These are words like *luxurious, foolproof, exclusive, urgent, tremendous, spectacular, monumental,* and *enormous.* These words trigger favorable or positive images in your listeners' minds. For example:

We can offer you exclusive rights and enormous savings if you are able to decide by Thursday.

Dynamic words: These are words like *rugged, power, speed, fast, quick, provocative, vibrant, vivid, rousing, seductive, alluring, spicy, racy, heady,* and *bold.* Excite or stimulate your listener. To stir emotions, you could say:

This new model has rugged power. It's fast, it's exciting to drive, and its racy look will arouse envy in all your friends.

Personal words. Words like *you, me, I, we, our,* and *your* help build a relationship with your customer. Usually they are parts of phrases like:

This saves *you* time because …

Our staff is waiting to serve *you.*

We make it easier for *you.*

We're in business to help *your* business succeed.

Personal words and phrases help to build a bond between you and your customers, implying that there is a partnership and that working with you is going to benefit them.

Most people like to hear their own names. They like to know that you are interested in them personally, not just in their wallets. Using someone's name helps to personalize your selling relationship and connect you with your customer.

Expressive, dynamic, and personal words are essential to effective sales communication. Develop and use emotional words to paint pictures, create images, and build relationships.

Use emotional words carefully. Sometimes they can trigger a response that completely stops the progress of the sale. The salesperson who criticizes competitors may turn a customer off completely. Or, if the prospect is the kind of person who likes to think things over, and the salesperson says, "You can't delay—you must act now— this is your only chance," the prospect may easily decide to pass up this wonderful opportunity because the stress of a decision is too overwhelming.

One person's treasured heirloom is just junk to someone else. And if you refer to "the good old days," you might activate memories of poverty, illness, and struggle. Words like *sleek, slinky, slim, slender,* and *svelte* may be positive words to one customer, but negative to another who has had a loved one die of an eating disorder.

Words have a power greater than any dictator, stronger than any bomb or bullet, more eternal than the speakers themselves. Isn't that fantastic? It's truly amazing when you think about it. The words *fantastic* and *amazing* create an emotional response in most people. So do the words *spend, tax, invest,* and *gain.* Phrases like *please* and *thank you, I apologize,* and *I'm sorry* can convey actions while triggering emotional responses.

USE COLORFUL WORDS

What images do your words create? Are they colorful, interesting, and memorable? Use words that your customers will understand from their own experiences, and be sure you touch their emotions. Try saying:

- Taste the excitement!
- Indulge yourself …
- Relax! You're safe with …
- Hot, fast, irresistible!

It's pleasing, rewarding, gorgeous, fascinating, enticing, inviting, ravishing, seductive, sexy, sleek, huggable, cuddly, adorable, exquisite, enthralling, congenial, perfect, enormous, gigantic, tremendous, spectacular, generous, lavish, and great, not to mention lovable. You'll be darn lucky to get it because it is rare, priceless, irreplaceable, extraordinary, amazing, phenomenal, remarkable, singular, stunning, and unique. And, best of all, it comes in tea rose, astronaut blue, race-stripe red, sparkling burgundy, blazing ruby, sensuous scarlet, burnt orange, frosted tangerine, sunny lemon, hot pink, goldenrod, tender turquoise, dollar green, ivory, alabaster, ebony, and burnished gold.

See how your words and phrases can be colorful, interesting, and memorable to touch the emotions? People decide more with their hearts than they do with their heads. When you speak, you want to create vivid pictures in the minds of your listeners. Help them see what they hear. Take the images in your mind, shape them into words, and use those words to convey the images into your customers' minds. Use power phrases, including words designed to soothe, lull, and calm when that is your goal. Send a clear message.

USE POWER WORDS

Some years ago, news commentator and language researcher Edwin Newman gave a speech full of examples of linguistic gobbledygook. He mentioned an educator who referred to writing as "articulating on paper," and vocabulary became "new word acquisition." Newman gave an example of someone discussing defenses against terrorism who said, "We need concerted, collective international effort with meaningful sanctionary teeth." Does that mean we should make biting comments?

Mr. Newman noted that in health-care jargon, deaths are "negative patient outcomes." And, tongue in cheek, he predicted that future marriage vows might read: "We will take each other for richer or poorer, in sickness and in health, until negative patient outcome do we part." Euphemisms are rarely power phrases.

How many powerful, emotional words or phrases can you tie to your goods or services? Get out a thesaurus or dictionary and make a list of words that will help you convey meaning and emotion.

Start with the letter "a." There are some very powerful words under "a:" *ability, abundant, achieve, active, admire, advantage, advance, affluence, amusement, affection, ambition, appreciation, appetite, approve, aspire, attain, attractive,* and *authoritative*. You can do that with every letter of the alphabet.

Compile the words that will motivate interest in what you sell. What about *beauty, benefit, capable, children, clean, comfort, desirable, deserving, determined, easy, effective, efficient, elegant, excellent, exceptional, fun, future, fate, fitting, genuine, good, grateful, handsome, honest, hospitality, imagination, improvement,* and *independent*? Are you beginning to get the idea? Soon you'll have a sales vocabulary second to none. Imagine how many powerful words you'll have if you tie your product to the whole alphabet from a to z.

In spare moments, rummage through magazines, newspapers, brochures, and catalogs to see what advertising copywriters are saying. Keep an open ear for compelling phrases you hear in TV and the radio spots. Jot them down in a notebook. Build your own treasure trove of words and phrases that work for you throughout your selling career. I've been selling, consulting on sales, and training salespeople for 41 years, and I'm still looking for new ways to say things.

Here are some real power phrases that you can use in your sales communications to capture attention:

- We must act now or lose the chance.
- You can count on me to help.
- This could be the best decade of the century.
- This guarantees a lifetime of satisfaction.
- Your decision could mean the difference between failure and success.
- If you've been waiting for the right moment, this is it!

USE CONNECTING WORDS

Compliment your listeners. Make sure they know they are important. Etiquette isn't entirely dead. Our more casual modern manners don't mean abandoning courtesy. Say, "It's my pleasure to help" or "I'll be glad to take care of that for you." Match your positive tone with positive words.

My wife Sheila and I bought a small item in a San Francisco store recently. We had almost reached the door when we heard a shout: "Wait! You! Come back here!" We turned to see the clerk waving frantically at us to return to the counter. She grabbed the bag from my hand, pulled out the sales receipt, and wrote "Thank You" across it in big letters. "We have to do that," she said sullenly. "Our new manager insists that we let the customer know we appreciate their business." That's an extreme example, but too many times I've encountered supposedly professional salespeople whose attitude was "take it or leave it." Given an option, I leave it.

Positive messages require sincerity. The words you use should express your expectation of a partnership, of a relationship, of a favorable business transaction. If you have expectation in your voice and use positive words, your listener will pay closer attention to your proposition.

One salesperson I know keeps a diary of all the good things he's communicated to others in the past week. He also makes a list of all the good things that were communicated to him, not just by customers, but by everybody he's talked to—family, friends, business acquaintances, even strangers. He goes over the list to see what words made the communication a "good" experience. Were there dramatic phrases, stories to illustrate a point? Did the person use expressive words, action words, descriptive words? What was said to impact both the mind and the emotions? He then tries to implement what he's learned in his sales interviews.

Because all action comes from ideas, and ideas are expressed by words and tone of voice, using clear words and a positive tone will give you a much better chance of closing a sale. Words are your tools. They can influence, persuade, or bully. They can inflame, calm, instruct, entertain, inspire, or motivate. And, yes, they can even get your customer to buy more. So use words not only to transmit facts, feelings, and opinions, but also attitudes, values, and beliefs.

BE HONEST

More important than your words, your emotions, and your tone is the honesty of what you're saying. Nothing can compensate for not speaking the truth.

An old Islamic proverb says that each word should pass through three gates before we say it. At the first gate, the gatekeeper asks, "Is it true?" At the second gate, "Is it necessary?" And at the third gate, "Is it kind?" Keep asking yourself if your message is true, necessary, and kind.

Never use phrases like, "to tell you the truth," "to be perfectly honest," or "trust me on this." Just tell the truth.

Also, don't make overstatements or use words like "always," "never," "everyone," or "no one." Such absolutes are rarely true.

Try to say, "and" instead of "but." "But" erases everything that went before it. It is an argumentative word, particularly when you're talking to a customer. "I know you think that you know what you're doing, *but* I know better." The word "but" should be avoided most of the time.

A better way to phrase the sentence above would be, "I know you think that you know what you're doing, *and* I agree, you do. Together we can form a partnership that can solve any challenge you have in this company."

BE SINCERE

The great comedian George Burns says, "Sincerity is the secret of success. Once you can fake that, you've got it made." Actually, it is nearly impossible to fake much with your customer. It is much better to study, practice, and master good sales presentation skills so that you can be a sincere and valuable resource to your prospects, customers, and clients.

AVOID CONFUSION

Words often mean different things to different people. Nido Qubain, a well-known speaker and trainer, points out, "The five most common words in the English language have more than 14,000 meanings." For example, "trunk" can mean a tree truck, an elephant's trunk, a car trunk, a torso, or a piece of luggage. Railways and telephones have trunk lines, and a particular ship's passageway and a number of mechanical devices are referred to as "trunks." Use words that can't be misunderstood in context.

My wife Sheila is also a professional speaker. On a rare occasion, we found it possible to travel together to separate speaking engagements, and we were driving down a road near Orlando, Florida. "Oh, look!" I said, "We're entering Kissimmee, Florida." I pronounced it KISS-a-mee.

"No," Sheila corrected me, "it's pronounced kis-SIM-ee."

We were having a typical family discussion, KISS-a-mee or kis-SIM-ee, when we realized it was lunch time, and we were hungry. We stopped at the next roadside restaurant. As we entered, I marched up to the cash register, smiling triumphantly, and asked the cashier, "Would you say very clearly where we are?"

She leaned forward and said very slowly, "Burg - er - King."

Obviously, I had been misunderstood.

Another time, just after Sheila and I had bought a new Jaguar, she phoned me and said, "Honey, I took the car to the car wash, and it broke down. The man is working on it with a sledge hammer."

"Stop him," I screamed, "You can't fix a car with a sledge hammer!"

She laughed. "He isn't working on the car, he's working on the car wash."

If you want to connect with your customer, say what you mean and be sure your listener understands what you say. Confirm that you are connecting by checking periodically for understanding.

The fanciest words in the world won't do you any good if you're not understood. Don't learn words and phrases just to impress people. Choose the ones that have meaning when applied to your product. Avoid slang words, buzzwords, acronyms, or technical terms unless you're positive your listener understands and prefers them.

Just the other day I received a phone call from a salesperson. It went like this: "This is B.G. Johnson, with ALA. I was just checking to see if you ever have reason to use our TQM training. Now, we cover TQS, TQI, TQE, and TQL."

I said, "huh?"

He said, "You know what I mean—total quality service, total quality improvement, total quality excellence, and total quality leadership. I'd like an appointment to tell you more. Can I get an affirmative on that?" Not only did he not get an affirmative, he got total silence. I didn't know what he was talking about. What did B.G. stand for? What was ALA? I had no idea what all this TQ-stuff he was talking about was or how it would apply to my business. In fact, I think he probably had a wrong number.

When you are presenting your product or service, follow these rules:

- Be clear.
- Be simple.
- Be understood.

Keeping your message clear and simple means not complicating your interaction with other people. Keep it simple. Remember, the Declaration of Independence has only 1,322 words. The Lord's Prayer has 56 words, and the song "We Shall Overcome," which moved millions during the civil rights struggle, has only 12 words. Obviously it does not take a lot of talk to have an impact on your customer.

During the Civil War, a famous speaker named Edward Everett spoke for one-and-a-half hours at the dedication of a cemetery for Union soldiers. He was followed by another speaker, Abraham Lincoln, who gave what is known as the Gettysburg Address. Just 268 words that are still remembered 100 years later by all who hear them. So, it doesn't take a lot of words to make your point, just the ability to say it the right way.

WORDS IN ACTION

Every customer is thinking, "What's in it for me?" You can't just describe what your product will do. You must show specifically how the customer will benefit. You need to answer the "What's in it for me?" question by following the AIDA formula. Every sale goes through four steps, for which AIDA forms a handy acronym:

Attention ("What is it?")

Interest ("I like it.")

Desire ("I want it.")

Action ("I'll take it.")

One of the best ways for novice salespeople to learn the subtleties of the AIDA formula is to study radio and TV commercials. Forgo your trip to the refrigerator or bathroom next time the commercials come on and pay close attention. After all, some of the greatest sales brains in the world are working in advertising, creating those commercials.

As you watch and listen, analyze the commercials, both good and bad. Ask yourself the questions from the checklist in Exhibit 4.1. Almost invariably, every commercial follows the AIDA formula. By studying how advertisers do it and adapting their techniques, you'll build connecting skills.

Exhibit 4.1
Ad Analysis Checklist

What type of commercial is this?

Is it entertaining?

Is it informative?

Is it persuasive?

What techniques are used to get attention?

Does the spokesperson or voice-over shout?

Does the advertisement use an authority figure to build credibility?

If it is a TV commercial, how do the visuals relate to the product?

Is there a lot of action and movement?

Does it use fallacious reasoning or questionable statistics?

Does it tie its product to one of the primary motivations?

If so, which motivation(s)? (Remember the five Ps.)

Profit

Peace of mind

Pleasure

Pain (freedom from)

Pride/self-esteem

Did this appeal work on you?

Were you motivated to take action? If not, why not?

Characterize the best and worst qualities of this commercial with a few adjectives:

USE LEGENDARY STORIES

Personalize your examples, anecdotes, and stories. Relate them as much as possible to your customer's personal experiences. Speaking is more effective when there are verbal illustrations that back up what you are trying to convey. I call this technique telling legendary tales.

You can find legendary tales in everyday experiences. I had one this week. I received my American Express credit card statement and I noticed that there was a $20 late fee. Since I always pay the card in full on time, I phoned American Express. The service agent looked up my account and told me that, two months earlier, I had (accidentally) sent a check for $50 less than my total balance, which triggered the late fee. However, she added quickly, "I see you've been an American Express cardholder since 1978 and you've never been late on a payment before, so I'm going to waive the $20 fee." I told her she really didn't have to do that, since it was really my mistake. She replied, "It is our pleasure at American Express to show appreciation to our best customers."

That is a legendary story of great service. It is a personal experience, and one that every person with a credit card or credit account can identify with.

What exceptional function has your product done for someone? What outstanding service have you or your company provided? When I'm doing seminars, I always ask the salespeople in the audience these questions. This is a new idea to them, and most can't think of a story at first. But after a little prodding, every audience comes up with some truly legendary experiences.

Recently I was speaking to a group that sold amplifiers for musical instruments. One of the salespeople told about a guitarist who was packing up his guitars and amplifiers quite late at night after a gig. He was loading them into the side door of a van parked next to the road, when suddenly a passing car caught an amplifier on the edge of its bumper and dragged it 100 feet. The amplifier case was totally destroyed, but when the amplifier was hooked up, it still worked. That was four years ago, the salesperson told us, and the guitarist is still using that same amp. Isn't that a great legendary story about quality?

What stories can you tell? Can you open the door to your customers' minds with stories about your exceptional product or service? Keep track of personal experiences that make a point, that can influence or persuade. Keep a notebook and fill it with legendary stories, then share these stories with your customers. Be ready to answer their unspoken questions:

- **Who else** has benefited from this product or service?
- **Who says so?**

Just because you, the salesperson, say that your product or service can do the job doesn't mean that your customers are convinced. Use convincing success stories.

USE SHOW AND TELL

Remember that we are a visually oriented society. Television, movies, computer screens—we're always looking at something. So when you tell your story, say it so it can be seen. Seeing is believing. Create external visuals as well as internal ones when it is appropriate. Do a "show and tell" presentation. Use charts, graphs, props, slides, overheads, flip charts, video presentations, or samples of your product. Show the item and then tell about it.

Sometimes we can see our own internal mental pictures more clearly than the actual external illustrations. As you connect, you will be creating strong mental images, both internally through words and ideas and externally through illustrations and demonstrations. Each of your prospects will process the information in different ways. Some people are primarily auditory, some visual, and some kinesthetic. You need to appeal to all three.

When Debbie Fields started selling cookies, she would walk down the street in Palo Alto, California, giving out samples. She had the cookies beautifully arranged on a silver tray, and she'd ask each passerby, "Wouldn't you like to taste one of my cookies?" The smell of freshly baked cookies and the taste were certainly kinesthetic. And the beauty of cookies bulging with chocolate chips, lying on a silver tray, certainly had a visual impact. Add to that her verbal questions and descriptions of the cookies. She addressed prospective customers in all three ways you must appeal to people: auditorally, visually, and kinesthetically. Debbie Fields has become one the most successful cookie sellers in history with her chain of Mrs. Fields' stores.

Another salesperson who knew how to convey kinesthetic imagery was dance instructor Arthur Murray. You've probably seen one of his footprint diagrams for doing the latest dance, each footprint numbered in sequence. One-two-three-slide-dip. Doesn't it look easy? Don't you want to try it?

You don't have to have actual physical objects to appeal to the visual and kinesthetic senses. You can do so through your choice of your examples and your stories. We're all very good at explaining what we want, but the examples we use have more impact. Make your story fit your point.

PAINT MENTAL PICTURES

Sally Henderson is the director of convention sales for the San Francisco Convention and Visitors Bureau, and she is an exceptional salesperson. When I asked her how she persuades large associations and corporations to hold their conventions and conferences in San Francisco, she said that she tries to create an irresistible picture in the minds of her prospects:

Have you ever ridden one of San Francisco's cable cars that go "half way to the stars?" That's just one of the many possible activities for your members if you hold your meeting in San Francisco.

Remember those pictures of the Golden Gate Bridge that you've seen? Well, the real view is even more spectacular. You'll be totally charmed by the Fisherman's Wharf area, Union Square, and all of the other things that make San Francisco unique.

Even more important, if you're using this conference as a profit-maker for your association, just having it in San Francisco will increase attendance because San Francisco itself is a big drawing card. It is one of the most popular cities to visit in the entire world. This year we've had conventions for (she names corporations and associations who have enjoyed the city.)

You'll be a real hero with those who attend your conference. That's what has happened to other meeting planners who picked San Francisco. Some of them even got standing ovations.

That's the outline of Sally's talk. Sometimes she does-
n't have to give it all because she watches the reactions of
her prospects. When she identifies which idea is creating
a response, she restates, reviews, reinforces, and finally
"futurizes" it with statements like:

- Why don't we plan how your group can have
  just as much fun while they're in San Francisco
  as other conventions have had?
- What activities will your employees be most
  interested in?
- Do you think they would enjoy tours to the wine
  country or the Monterey Aquarium?
- What about the golf course at Pebble Beach?
- You'll be just a few blocks from Union Square
  and some superb shopping. Will that appeal to
  family members who come along?
- There are a dozen world-famous restaurants
  within a few blocks of the hotel you're going to
  book. Would you like a list? Some require
  advance reservations, so you may want to plan
  ahead.
- Can't you just see all those thank-you letters
  you'll get after the conference is over?

The prospects are already munching on fresh crab
and feeling the fog in their faces as they plummet down
Russian Hill toward the Bay on the side of a cable car.

SELL THE SIZZLE

Human decisions are based on logic, right? If you believe this, look around. Everything we do is related in some way to our personal interests. Even our most selfless actions on behalf of others repay us with personal satisfaction and a feeling of self-worth.

Your job is to provide each customer with the answer to the unspoken question, "What will this do for me?"

Selling starts with features and benefits. Nearly all salespeople have heard that mantra: Features and benefits, features and benefits, features and benefits. Every training session tries to drum the basics of features and benefits into every salesperson's consciousness. But, as we discussed in Step One, a professional salesperson connects with the customer by adding a third tool: personal motivation. "What's in it for me? How will this make my life better?"

Let's say you come to my office to sell me a computer and you tell me that the model you suggest is a 486 VX2/66 with 8 megabytes of ram, two sizes of floppies, a 340-meg hard disk, and a 1024 by 768 monitor on a 15" screen. Those are the features. But, I'm really computer illiterate. I have no interest whatsoever in what the computer is or what the hardware has built in. What I want to know about is benefits. What does it do?

So, if you're going to connect with me, you will show me how I'm going to get more for less. You might say things like:

- This is the one that does the best for less.
- You can expect a 50 percent increase in performance over your current computers.

- It's designed to make upgrades a snap.
- It displays Windows up to four times faster.
- We offer round-the-clock technical support, with a toll-free number 24 hours a day, seven days a week. We also guarantee, in writing, that you will receive a fast response from our technical experts whenever you call us with a problem or a question.

Those are the benefits—what the computer does. But the real selling point is the motivation. What does it do for me? You might tell me something like:

> *This computer is designed for both the expert and the novice. Whatever your level of expertise, you will find that this model makes your work easier, faster, more productive, more professional, and more profitable. It gives you an advantage over the competition because it will give you more power, and less trouble, at a lower price.*

That is *motivation*. Your customers are looking for benefits, not features. Sometimes they are sophisticated enough to know which features will give them the benefits they want: "I need a printer with more than 300 dpi, a parallel interface, and a paper tray that holds at least one ream of paper." But don't count on them doing the work for you. Use artful questioning to determine their needs and what motivates those needs. Transform a feature into a benefit and from there, via the emotions, into the answer of your prospect's spoken or unspoken need.

People don't buy BTUs or R factors. They buy lower energy bills and the comfort of a home that's not too hot or too cold. They don't buy insurance or cemetery plots. They buy peace of mind. They don't buy color TVs. They buy the information, pleasure, and relaxation of sitting after a hard day's work and watching their favorite sit-com. People don't buy automobiles. They buy the convenience and freedom of getting where they want to go, the power of living and working where they choose without those choices being dictated by public transportation. They buy the thrill of speed, the pleasure of luxurious interiors and surroundings, and the prestige of owning a status symbol.

You're not selling things. You're selling ideas, concepts, feelings, self-esteem, self-confidence, and pleasure. The great sales teacher Elmer Wheeler said, "Always sell the sizzle, not the steak." But in fact, when you connect with your customer, you sell both. The formula is still L+R+E=S (Logic plus Reason plus Emotion equals success.)

What are the positives and negatives of what you're selling? Could this product be used in ways the producer never imagined? How will you prove this feature will benefit your customers, solve their problems, fill their needs, fulfill their desires, and fix what's wrong? That's your goal: to fix the problem.

A SUCCESS STORY

The 3M Scotch tint window film is a coating that can be installed inside your windows to reflect most of the sun's radiant heat. It blocks 74 percent to 99 percent of the sun's ultraviolet rays and still lets the light in. I'm sure there are other brands besides 3M, but this particular product made a big difference to a friend of mine who had opened a very plush restaurant. The building had enormous windows all along the south side of the dining room with a great view for his customers. He purchased expensive carpeting and table coverings and decorated the walls with oil paintings. All this was okay at night, but the lunch crowd complained about the heat and glare from the direct sunlight. My friend had a big problem.

Luckily, a salesperson decided that he could help my friend solve his problem. He started by pointing out the investment that my friend had in the furniture, carpets, draperies, wallpaper, fabrics, and almost irreplaceable photographs and artwork. He went on to say that the windows could be covered with drapes or blinds, but they would block the beautiful view and create a closed-in feeling.

However, with his "sun control" window film on the windows, the customers and the owner could both win. The film would insulate the windows while leaving the view. The furniture and fabrics would have a longer life. Glare would be reduced. It would also stay cooler, therefore saving money on air conditioning. And the best thing about the product was that the cost was much lower than drapes, blinds, or other types of window coverings. He also pointed out that the product had a five-year warranty that fully covered the entire cost of replacement if it proved defective in any way. Now, wasn't that a solution to the problem?

Treat the cause not the symptom. Fix the problem, never the blame. Never tell your prospects that they're doing something wrong. Instead, offer proof that your product or service can do it better. Sometimes these proofs are simply logical assumptions. Sometimes they're based on asking prospects to respect and trust the past reputation of the product or service. Sometimes you need a demonstration.

Start by understanding the customer's desires and expectations, then match the product's true benefits to the buyer's true needs. This is connecting with your customer.

KNOWLEDGEABLE OR KNOW-IT-ALL?

Know everything that you possibly can about your product or service and your customer. But, after you've worked hard to acquire this exhaustive compendium of knowledge, you will be greatly tempted to show off—and you absolutely must not. Resist the impulse to rattle off lists of technical information. This will be hard to do. How could anyone *not* be fascinated by all these wonderful details that you worked so hard to memorize, all these features the engineers have incorporated into your product, and all the scientific supports for your process?

Easily! Imagine that you're consulting a doctor about a rash and you get a lecture on skin diseases. Soon the doctor is striding excitedly back and forth, enumerating dozens of potential treatments and outcomes, totally engrossed in proving to you what a brilliant medical education can do. You and your rash are no longer center stage. How do you feel? Well, that's just how a prospective customer feels when you are intent on impressing, dazzling, and proving your own importance.

Instead of proving how important you are, concentrate on proving how important your customer is. Keep the spotlight on your buyer's motivations.

My daughter Julie recently bought a new home. She and her husband had decided to consult a professional landscaper about fixing up the back yard. Julie told me that her main concerns were shade, color, and low maintenance. I was there when the consultant arrived. He introduced himself as a landscape architect, and he told us that this was quite different from being a landscape planner or a landscape gardener. He said his training would enable him to make better selections than any competitor. As he walked around the back yard, he pointed to one spot and said, "A nice *acacia pendula* could go here." At another corner, he said, "A trio of *bettula nigra* would be very nice here. And near the back fence a *cornus florida* would be just perfect. Against the garage wall, we need to plant *hedera*. Along the side fence, *calistenon citrinus*, and for the hillside beyond the fence, *delosperma alba*."

His confidence, manner, and vocabulary were most impressive, but I was watching my daughter, and she was totally lost. I interrupted him and said, "Could you please tell us all this in plain, simple English so we can understand?" He gave me a condescending smile and said, "Well, yes. The *acacia pendula* is an acacia tree with beautiful yellow blooms in the spring and early summer. The *bettula nigra* is a birch tree. We would have three of them over in that corner. The *cornis florida* is a flowering dogwood, and it would be just perfect in the middle of the yard near the back fence. On the garage wall, we'd put the *hedera* which is ivy, but it's a clinging ivy that will grow up and cover the wall. Then *calistenon citrinus* is simply bottle brush. It's very easy to grow, needs little water, and nothing can destroy it. Finally, on the hillside we will put *delosperma alba*, which is ice plant."

My daughter still looked uncertain. "All I want is shade, color, and low maintenance. Can we get that?" This expert had been "selling" for half an hour and she had no idea if what he was suggesting was what she wanted.

Your first job in connecting with your customers is to discover what they want, then tell them how they can get it in terms they will understand and be excited about.

10 STEPS TO THE SALE

Once you've ascertained your customers' needs and desires, the basic steps of a successful sales presentation rarely vary.

1. Start by promising a benefit.
2. Elaborate with an example.
3. Explain how that example fits into your customers' personal needs and experiences.
4. Ask more questions to be sure that you understand the need or problem and that your customers are aware of it as well.
5. Show how what you're selling has helped other people, and relate what they have said about it.
6. Apply the benefits to a very specific problem the prospect has, and back up your statement with proof.
7. Show how a loss could occur if your product or service is not purchased.
8. Ask to be sure that the prospect understands.
9. Re-emphasize the benefits and the personal motivations.
10. Ask for the order.

These are the elements of a good sales presentation. You may use technical drawings, statistics, or lists of features to get your message across, but use them to build powerful mental images of what buyers can do with this feature. Otherwise, they might substitute their image of what's wrong with your product for your image of what's good about it.

THE SO-BECAUSE RULE

Before you have your next sales contact, make a list of features and potential benefits and motivations for your customer. As you design your approach or presentation, think of questions you can use to emphasize the perceived benefits of each feature and try to tie the features and benefits together.

You do this with two key words: "so" and "because." This simply means that if you start by describing a feature, continue with the word "so," and then show how that feature produces a benefit. For example:

This weather proofing can be sprayed on with a garden sprayer, *so* it is much easier to apply and clean up.

If you start with a benefit, follow it with the word "because," and mention the feature.

This waterproofing is easy to apply and clean up *because* it is made to be used with an ordinary garden sprayer.

Your pattern is:

You get these benefits *because* of these features.
It has these features, *so* you get these benefits.

ANALYZING YOUR SPEAKING SKILLS

If you want to analyze your speaking skills in sales situations, ask yourself these eight questions:

1. **How do I greet people, in person and on the telephone?** There's nothing worse than picking up a phone and hearing a dead voice on the other end. How do you answer the phone? How about in person? Do you extend your hand? Do you smile? Do you say, "Nice to meet you?" Do you greet people with a positive first thought? Do you use the words that trigger their emotions?

2. **Does your face know how you feel?** I've met people who just don't let their faces know how they feel. They may be excited, but you'd never know it by the way they look. Even if you don't feel your best, try to put forward the best face you can.

3. **Do you interrupt when someone else tries to speak?** It took me a long time to get over the habit of interrupting. In fact, I'm not sure that I'm over it yet. But I have conquered a good part of it in my business life because I'm aware that if I interrupt I very well may lose the sale. It's a very difficult habit to break if you think fast and the other person talks slowly. But work on it!

4. **Do I speak clearly, slowly, and concisely?** Often people are not able to listen as fast as you can talk. You need to stop, pause, and give them a chance to absorb what you are saying. The pause is one of the most important techniques of sales communication. It

emphasizes, gives the other party time to think, adds drama, gives the listener time to catch up, and gives you time to decide if your customers are really listening. It's a valuable tool.

5. Am I aware of the tone and pitch of my voice? Is it pleasant? Often when salespeople get enthusiastic, their voices get higher and higher. And higher. The higher the voice, the harder it is to listen. Lower your voice. People understand more when listening is a pleasant experience.

6. Do I exaggerate? This is a death knell for modern, sensitive, and service-oriented salespeople. Sell, don't oversell. Don't exaggerate yourself, your product, or your company. Just tell the truth. It's amazing how effective truth is in communicating what you want other people to know.

7. Am I good at remembering names? Psychologists tell us that the word we most love to hear is our name. Remembering names helps you communicate and fosters understanding. If you're not good at remembering a name, repeat it, write it down, and reread it. Ask the person to pronounce it again. Keep working at it until you get it clear in your mind. Look at your written note of your customer's name so you'll remember.

8. How do I say good-bye? Goodbye is an important part of sales communication. How you end your conversation with your customer or prospect affects your next encounter.

My dear friend and long-time associate Goldie Long was an expert at saying good-bye at the end of a sales interview. Goldie had a routine that never varied, whether she had made the sale or not. Her sincerity, warmth, and skill made every customer or prospect feel good about being with her, and they looked forward to her returning. Goldie was selling personal development training, and her routine went something like this:

> First, I want to thank you for the time you've given me today. I know that time is the most valuable asset that anyone has, and I truly appreciate you sharing it with me. Second, I would really like to compliment you on your personal development. Whatever program you've been following has certainly helped you develop as a caring, concerned, kind human being. But they say, "It's not the destination that's important, it's the journey through life." If I can be a resource to you or help you in any way in reaching your personal development goals, please feel free to call on me. It would truly be my pleasure to serve you.

With that, Goldie shook her customer's hand, turned, and went to the door. I have never met anyone who didn't look forward to a return visit from Goldie.

A skilled speaker uses words like a magician uses props. Everything that good sales communicators do, from precall planning to follow-up, is designed to win over the client, customer, or prospect. You connect with your customers with clear, persuasive speech.

STEP FIVE

CROSS THE BARRIERS (HOW DO YOU OVERCOME CULTURE, GENDER, AND AGE CONSIDERATIONS?)

Recently, while traveling on United Airlines, I was reading the instruction card in the seat pocket. It said, "If you are sitting in an exit row and you cannot understand this card or cannot see well enough to follow these instructions, please tell a crew member." The problem of course, is that if you couldn't understand the card, you wouldn't know to tell a crew member.

Thishis leads us to one of the fundamental barriers to connecting with the customer: How do you communicate when you can't understand others and they can't understand you? Sales communication is difficult enough, but connecting with people from very different cultural, occupational, and educational backgrounds, geographical areas, age groups, and even genders is a major challenge in today's diverse society. Good communicators don't take the easy way out, by selling only to PLM (people like me). They work constantly to expand their awareness and skills beyond their personal environment and experience.

BASICS OF SELLING TO ANYONE

Fortunately most of the rules for connecting to someone who is different are the same for just about everyone. Let's start by reviewing these basics.

1. RESPECT your customer.
2. Ask questions, then listen to the answers so you fully and completely understand the customer's needs, desires, and expectations.
3. Make customers feel relaxed and willing to share their thoughts with you.
4. Build relationships with potential customers that allow you to be trusted, respected, and liked.
5. Learn to present information to potential customers in the way they are most able to receive it.
6. Make it easy for them to buy from you.

If you assume that everyone else in the world thinks and reacts exactly as you do—or *should*—your power to connect will be drastically limited. How can you develop communication skills for a broad customer base with different needs and expectations? Constant discovery and adaptation are necessary to bridge the barriers. Learn to persuade in a variety of different styles rather than forcing one style on all people. You can do this without surrendering your personal uniqueness. Be yourself, but be sensitive to others.

Diversity is a reality of business life. Maybe you've never attended the services of another religion, attended an ethnic festival, or studied world history. Maybe you're not aware that the cultures of Japan, China, and Korea are as different as those of Ireland, Denmark, and Poland, even though the former are all Asians and the latter are all Europeans. Perhaps you've never played golf at a country club or stick ball on a city street, camped out in the wilderness or ridden a crowded subway at rush hour. Maybe you've never stood for five hours in high heels, sat for five hours in a wheelchair, or worn a suit and tie on a 100-degree day. Still, you as a salesperson must constantly search your own mental databank for insights into how these experiences have affected the lives and perceptions of your potential customers.

GEOGRAPHICAL DIFFERENCES

At one time in my selling career, I was working in Mississippi. I grew up in California, and at first I had trouble communicating with my customers. Mississippians seemed to talk more slowly and use lots of colloquial phrases that were incomprehensible to me. Sometimes they were so polite I didn't realize I hadn't gotten a sale.

Another time I worked in New York, and that was just as hard. New Yorkers seemed to be quicker, more abrupt, and "in your face." They constantly interrupted, and it took me a while to figure out that meant they agreed rather than disagreed.

So, if you're from California and you're selling in New York, you need to be more assertive in your communication style than you usually are. And if you're a New Yorker selling in California, soften your approach and "mellow out." If you're selling in the southern states, just remember that your customers are not slow thinkers or uninformed. They just speak more slowly.

Each geographical area has a different style of communicating. To fine-tune your approach, read local newspapers, listen to local radio stations, and watch local television. Identify the differences, then adjust your approach to your prospects.

DIFFERENT OCCUPATIONAL BACKGROUNDS

Recently, I did a sales seminar for a company named Coherent that manufactures medical lasers. To gather information to custom-tailor my presentation, I interviewed three of their salespeople. Now, I've always thought I was a pretty good listener and prided myself on my vocabulary, but these people kept me on my toes! Every third word was a technical term, and I found it took me twice as long as usual to gather the information I needed. I was forced to interrupt frequently to ask what some of the terms meant.

Obviously, the more education and technical training you can get, the better equipped you'll be to adapt your presentation to different audiences. Doctors, pastry chefs, machinists, and airplane pilots all have different nomenclature, lingo, and buzzwords. Study the terminology and industry jargon the same way you'd study a foreign language. Remember the expression for being in agreement: "Now you're talking my language." Literally talking someone's language is a great start to connecting.

People in different professions also can have very different demeanors and different expectations about how you should approach them. As a sensitive, caring professional, you will take your cues and clues from them and respond as they want you to respond. Use sensitive pacing and mirroring to put yourself in harmony with your prospects.

COMMUNICATING WITH OTHER CULTURES

The Caucasian male, long the standard American worker, is fast becoming an endangered species. By the year 2000, the Hudson Institute predicts (in its publication *Work Force 2000*) Caucasian males will make up only 15 percent of the new entrants into the workforce. The other 85 percent will be women and/or what are euphemistically called "minorities." (Most "minorities" are majorities in the larger global picture.)

WHAT'S WRONG WITH THE OLD WAY?

This book is mostly about "American" selling, but today that has to expand to include highly diverse customers. Traditional American customs can clash with those of other cultures. Much of the world sees Americans as impatient. Americans use direct and open communication, often seen as too brusque or blunt. Americans prefer working alone to working in teams, and their emphasis is on short-term goals and gains. They emphasize content over relationships, and often use a legalistic approach rather than an ethical one: "If it's not illegal, it's okay." And unfortunately many Americans have had few experiences with other cultures. All of these factors can be huge stumbling blocks when you want to connect with people from different backgrounds. What are normally considered "good communication strategies" may not work at all.

The secret to communicating is always to treat people as they wish to be treated. *Let them show you how they want you to connect.* Be sensitive to their comfort. Respond to their level of formality or casualness, reserve or exuberance, calmness or energy. At the slightest sign of discomfort, adjust your approach to try to achieve harmony.

BACK TO OUR ROOTS

America has always presented itself to the world as a "melting pot." When I was a child, I lived in a neighborhood made up of Irish, Germans, Italians, Jews, Greeks, and African-Americans. Each group was proud of its background, but, without exception, they wanted to fit into the larger picture of American culture. Even though some parents barely spoke English, their children were discouraged from speaking their parents' native tongue or learning the history of their ancestors. Very few parents tried to keep their heritage alive for their offspring.

Since then, the U.S. population has doubled. Perhaps the sheer volume is so overwhelming that people now want to identify with smaller, more manageable affinity groups. Universities are offering cultural heritage classes so people can rediscover their roots. America is becoming more of a mosaic and less of a melting pot. Eleven percent of the U.S. population speaks a language other than English at home.

The largest groups—African-Americans, Hispanics, Asians, and Middle Easterners—make up a tremendous and growing market. It is estimated that the first three of these groups are spending over $500 billion a year. This is a fantastic customer base with purchasing power that exceeds the gross national product of Canada. If you can't communicate with these diverse groups, you will lose that market. Diversity is here to stay. Success will depend on how well you develop your ability to function and communicate with extremely varied customers.

LANGUAGE BARRIERS

No group is monolithic. You can't appeal to a stereotype and be successful. Among the 25 million Hispanics, you can't even use the same Spanish words in different groups. For example, the word for "little boy" in Mexico is *chamoco*; in Guatemala, it is *patojo;* in El Salvador, *cipote*; in Cuba, *chico*; and in the Dominican Republic, *nio*.

Sondra Thiederman, author of *Profiting in America's MultiCultural Marketplace*, suggests that we be aware of the language diversity that exists in different groups, and that when language is a problem we follow these guidelines:

1. Be precise in your choice of words.
2. Avoid sounds that are difficult to decipher.
3. Speak slowly and enunciate clearly.
4. Minimize jargon, idioms, and slang.

5. Use short, uncomplicated sentences.
6. Keep it simple.
7. Use nonverbal signs to convey meaning.

To this list, I'll add: *Never* seem condescending or treat the customer like a child. The halting English you hear may be one of six or seven languages your prospect speaks. Before you smirk at any linguistic mistakes, ask yourself how well you can speak his or her native tongue.

ETIQUETTE DIFFERENCES

Etiquette can vary widely from culture to culture. Nevertheless, there are still some cross-cultural etiquette basics.

Never call people by their first names when you've just met them. This can be very insulting. And don't discuss personal subjects or assume a level of intimacy on short acquaintance. Formality is the safest course until you are invited to be more casual.

When my wife and I did seminars in Poland, we discovered that the Polish people are extremely formal. Everyone is called by their last name: Mr. Krepik or Mr. Bonacheck. This isn't unfriendly but a sign of respect. First names are used only by family members and intimate friends. So we had to remember to speak and listen in a much more formal manner than we normally do in the United States.

Most people born outside the United States favor formal behavior on first acquaintance. We Americans want to get to the point quickly, rush through the process, assume friendship, get delivery, and close the deal. This can be seen as rude, pushy, and disrespectful by other cultures. Good sales communicators match the pace of their customers, take time to build relationships their way, and follow the Chinese proverb: "Friendship first. Business second."

Sometimes, relaxing over a cup of coffee and *not* talking business has to come first. In Poland, we had more than 100 meetings with business and government leaders. At every single meeting, we were first invited to sit down for conversation over coffee and cookies. Only after some trust was established did we go on to the business at hand.

MORE CROSS-CULTURAL DON'TS

Although all cultures have different mores and require different communication techniques, some rules cross all cultural lines.

- **Never embarrass anyone.** No one wants to suffer embarrassment, and no one ever should. Concern for others' comfort is fundamental to any communication effort. Arguing, complaining, or ridiculing is a good way to end the conversation and the relationship.
- **Never criticize.** Some cultures require group decisions. Never criticize past actions or decisions because they will reflect on others and that could be humiliating. Always let people save face.
- **Never demand.** If you ask questions, ask respectfully. It's a good idea to explain why you are asking questions so you don't seem too aggressive.

- **Never seem impatient or disapproving when others speak haltingly.**
Watch faces to see if you are understood. When you think there's a problem, rephrase your statement. In fact, it's not a bad idea to restate main points in several ways. We Americans don't realize how idiomatic English can be. Everyday phrases like, "I'll catch up" or "I'll see it through" are confusing for people learning English. What is the correct response to "You can say that again?"

THE MINEFIELD OF CULTURAL MISUNDERSTANDINGS

Sometimes people are reluctant to ask questions because they don't want to appear ignorant. Maybe they are reluctant to complain about a lack of service, a product failure, or a price because they don't want to embarrass the salesperson. Or they may be reluctant to accept praise offered in public. Some are even reluctant to take advantage of special considerations or discounts, because in their culture this puts them in your debt.

Harvey Johnson, a friend of mine who sells automobiles, was attempting to sell a car to a Japanese couple. He told them all about the features and how these features would benefit them. The couple seemed to understand and to agree that they liked those features. He was sure they were saying yes to the sale, but at the end of the presentation they thanked him politely and left without buying. When Harvey and I discussed this particular interview, I pointed out that the Japanese prize harmony. They'd never want to seem disagreeable, even if they disagree.

We can never assume that our prospective customers negotiate exactly as we do, and this is especially true if they are from another culture. One of Harvey's mistakes was that he offered wire wheels, tinted glass, and other options without charge. In most sales situations, that would be a plus. But this couple, born in Japan and recently arrived in the United States, came from a culture where there is a reluctance to be honored or made especially important. One Japanese proverb says, "The nail that sticks up gets hammered down." Of course, this is not true for everyone born in Japan, especially those who have lived here for a number of years. But Harvey made a mistake because he didn't understand his customers. When you learn as much as you can about the cultures of your potential customers, you are better able to communicate on their level.

Some cultures wouldn't dream of offending you by saying "definitely not." With such customers, it is best not to ask closed-end questions. Use multiple choice instead. Chinese people dislike being patted, poked, or hugged. They admire patience and they expect you, the sales communicator, to show it. Most people from Mexico and Italy like to touch and expect you to be warm and personal in your communications. Good communicators follow the lead and match the style of the other person.

A good example is the handshake. Americans strive for a firm, purposeful handshake, but Middle Easterners and Asians prefer a gentler grasp. The French have a light touch; the Germans a tight, brusque grasp. The one gesture that seems common to all cultures is the smile. While far from universal, it is usually okay to use the smile to communicate good will.

Be careful with your body language when working with other cultural groups. Learn what are considered offensive gestures and avoid them. A raised index finger in much of Europe has the same meaning as a raised middle finger in the United States. The "okay" sign of thumb and forefinger together is unspeakably rude in Mediterranean countries where it symbolizes an anatomical orifice. We'll talk more about this in Step Nine, but for now remember that sometimes actions speak louder than words, and the body language you use may not mean what you want it to mean.

Recognize the differences within each cultural and ethnic group. Sondra Thiederman stresses that each person is unique, even though there may be some general cultural similarities. Not all Mexicans live in large, close-knit families; not all Italians are great singers, and not all French people are great chefs. Not all Japanese and Germans are technical geniuses. Thiederman says, "We don't have to be twins to be brothers.... Just because we are equal doesn't mean we are all the same." Good sales communicators are sensitive to the differences. But, the bottom line is most people have the same basic agendas. Regardless of cultural differences, what you want most in your heart is the same as what other people want.

COMMUNICATING WITH THE OPPOSITE SEX

Traditional American selling was usually white men selling to other white men. In 1993, women made up 45 percent of the workforce. Some statistics indicate they control 55 percent of our national economy. This means a lot more women are selling and a lot more women are buying. It follows that sooner or later, most salesmen will want to sell to women, and most saleswomen will want to sell to men. Even with rapidly changing sex roles in our society, cross-gender selling still presents some unique problems.

It's long been assumed that men and women "don't speak the same language." Some recent studies show that—whether because of genetics or social modeling—this is partially true.

Generally, men prefer to communicate on a nonpersonal basis. They avoid personal discussion and stick to exchanging details about public events. They gather together to solve the world's problems or to establish their status by discussing their accomplishments and skills, especially in sports. There's an old saying, "It's just business," and that seems to be more true for men than for women.

Women tend to communicate on a more personal level. They are interested in details and take things more personally. The National Foundation for Women Business Owners released a study in 1994 indicating that men think more in terms of hierarchy and established rules, whereas women tend to think of their businesses as family and their professional relationships as networks.

Women tend to emphasize intuitive thinking, stressing creativity and sensitivity. But most men (71 percent according to this study), stress logical thinking, which emphasizes analyzing and processing information and developing procedures for getting tasks done. Men's interest in politics, news, and sports parallels women's interest in personal details. For most women, getting together to discuss their lives is the heart of friendship.

Good communicators recognize that most female customers will want to socialize, however briefly, before getting down to business. It is also more common for women to show they're listening by making eye contact, smiling supportively, and nodding. In other words, they connect and bond.

DIFFERENT STROKES

Judith C. Tingley, Ph.D., in her book *Genderflex*, lists three major differences between men's and women's communication styles.

1. **Differences in content.** Men talk about money, sports, business. They deal in facts. Women talk about people, emotions, and relationships. They deal in feelings.
2. **Differences in style.** Men try to solve problems, fix what's wrong, and compete with each other to win. Women try to understand, support, and connect. Their style is more cooperative than combative.
3. **Differences in responses.** Men tend to get to the point quickly and answer questions without a lot of elaboration. ("How did the sales interview go?" "Fine.") Women, on the other hand, are more detailed.

My own observation is that women ask more questions during a sales interview, particularly confirming questions. They want to be understood and to be sure that they understand.

Tingley says that to do more business, we should all learn to choose and use communication patterns that are as similar as possible to those of the gender with which we are communicating. In other words, communicate on your customers' terms.

HOW MEN CAN CONNECT WITH WOMEN

Patricia Ball, a communications expert who lectures on sales communication, says that if a man wants to sell to women, he must do the following:

1. Admit that gender differences exist. Women want to be treated fairly, but not necessarily like one of the guys.
2. Examine yourself for stereotypical thinking. Don't assume that a woman is too weak to make a firm decision.
3. Explore the differences. Studies indicate that women listen more attentively than men, whereas men interrupt more than women. Women don't like aggressiveness or too much talk from a salesperson. Men generally use more sports terminology than women. Respect and adapt to gender differences without placing value judgments on them.

To these points, I'll add some of my own:

4. Reduce the quantity of references to business, money, and sports.
5. Add references to people, feelings, and relationships.
6. Use active listening skills.
7. Ask more than you tell. Ask how she feels about the product or service, then *listen* to her answers!
8. Never condescend or become familiar. Women don't like being addressed as if they were cute children, using first names without permission or diminutive pet names. A saleswoman at a

convention I attended wrote on her name tag:
"Hi, my name is Susan.
NOT HONEY!!

9. Avoid sexual humor.
10. Avoid aggressiveness. Stress service and partnership.
11. Use a win-win competitive style, not a win-lose
style.

HOW WOMEN CAN CONNECT WITH MEN

Women selling to men as equals and without traditional
"feminine wiles" requires some gentle reeducating for
both the female salesperson and the male customer. If a
woman wants to sell to a man, she could:

1. Reduce the quantity of references to people,
feelings, and relationships.
2. Add more references to business, money, and
particularly sports.
3. Use humor, but *not* self-effacing humor. Never
demean yourself.
4. Don't be irritated or defensive if a male client
strives for a win-lose outcome. Instead, concentrate on creating win-win solutions.
5. Be forceful and use power words. Don't soften
your approach with unnecessary disclaimers or
apologies. Men can interpret the hesitant
approach, which has traditionally been seen as
"ladylike" and "good mannered," as weak and
indecisive.
6. Be brief and specific. Say what needs to be
said. Ask permission to elaborate if you feel it's
necessary: "Shall I take a few minutes to

explain that to you?" "Would it help you to have some background on that?"

7. Be patient but firm with men who try to disconcert you and gain an advantage with traditional male power plays like sexual innuendoes, flattery, profanity, abuse, or condescension. Consider their education part of your job.

COMMUNICATING WITH OTHER AGE GROUPS

Everyone tends to communicate from their own experiences, and our experiences at different ages differ. Consider some of the most indelible events of this century. Fifty percent of the people alive today are too young to remember the assassination of President John F. Kennedy. Seventy percent don't remember a time when there was no television. Eighty-five percent are not old enough to remember the 1929 stock market crash that launched the Great Depression.

It is very difficult to talk across decades. Often the vocabulary is different. Language, especially slang, changes swiftly. "Bad" is good. "Cool" is hot. Suddenly "needy" refers to emotional immaturity, rather than poverty. Lately, when I say "thank you" to a younger person, they reply, "No problem." My mother brought me up to say, "You're welcome." (Some slang is geographical, not age-specific, but I've heard "no problem" from teenagers across the United States and in Australia.)

One of my sons speaks rap. Recently he told me:

If you want to sell me, and you think I'll buy,
Then start out by lookin' me straight in the eye.
Tell me your story. Mean what you say.

But make it quick. I ain't got all day.
If your product's good and your service is great,
Speak right up, don't hesitate.
Ask me a question. When I answer back,
Check to be sure you're on the right track.
Use your logic to make your appeal.
But also discover just how I feel.
I want to know what's in it for me.
Is the value I'm getting worth the fee?
Can you solve my problem, help me achieve?
If you think you can, make me believe.
Touch my mind and my heart too.
If you can do that, I'll buy from you.

I'm not suggesting that a good salesperson has to be able to rap to sell to younger people, but be aware of communication differences.

Older people often make references to things that younger people don't know about. I was talking to my 35-year-old son the other day about World War II and I mentioned "Kilroy." He kept nodding as if he understood, but some of his gestures made me a little bit suspicious. So I asked him, "Do you know who Kilroy was?"

He said, "No, was he a pilot?"

Anyone over age 50 knows that millions of GIs wrote "Kilroy was here" on every available surface in Europe, often adding a bulbous-nosed cartoon of this fictional character. But my reference was lost on a 35-year-old. Similarly, older people can feel like they've been dropped on another planet when younger people make references to the latest song hits or dance crazes.

Connecting with the elderly is a special skill. One day my 84-year-old mother made up her mind to buy an insurance policy. I decided to be with her when the salesperson called, just to be sure she wasn't taken advantage of. What a lesson I learned. This man was an absolute master at communicating with an older person. To start with, he was very solicitous of my mother's opinions. He listened to every word she said. He asked her what she wanted to happen at her funeral and wrote down her answers. Then he read her words back to her and asked if he had understood. He spoke slowly and distinctly. While he didn't shout, he spoke loudly enough for her to hear him clearly. He summarized all the points, estimated the costs, and explained how a monthly payment could purchase an insurance annuity that would accomplish her desires. I learned a lesson that day about how to connect with an older person.

The experiences of different age groups are also different. Some of us identify with the music of Glen Miller's Big Band, whereas others respond to Hammer. It's the same with motion pictures, books, and historical events. People who survived the Great Depression, the Holocaust, or the civil rights movement of the 1960s can have very different overall perceptions of the world than people who have never struggled or lacked for anything. The intensity of our group experiences are etched indelibly in our minds and emotions. Good sales communicators learn to relate to these memories and feelings, even if they have not had similar experiences.

George Bernard Shaw once said, "The greatest problem with communication is the illusion that it has been accomplished." Connecting across culture, gender, and age barriers takes extra effort and expertise, but it's worth it!

STEP SIX

USE INFLUENCE AND PERSUASION
(HOW DO YOU USE
FRIENDLY PERSUASION?)

My friend and fellow speaker Jim Tunney, former referee with the National Football League, was the after-dinner speaker at a banquet. Seated at the head table, Jim turned to the head waiter and asked for another pat of butter for his baked potato. The waiter said, "Sorry, sir, there's just one pat of better per customer." Jim said, "I guess you don't realize who I am. I refereed three

Super Bowls. I was in charge of those and am here tonight as the featured speaker for this banquet." "Yes, sir," the waiter replied, "I realize that, but maybe you don't know who I am." Jim said, "No, you've got me there." The waiter said, "I'm the man in charge of the butter."

Different people control different situations. A good salesperson connects with customers by influencing the person currently in control. A good example is when an assistant is trying to protect the boss: "May I tell her what this call is about? She's a very busy woman." The assistant is almost totally in control.

What can you do to influence people to help you achieve your goals and objectives? What powers do you have to encourage cooperation? Some people use the power of force, some the power of position, and some the power of personal persuasion.

THE POWER OF FORCE

Al Capone said that you get much further with a kind word and a gun than with a kind word alone. That may be true if you are alone with your victim in a dark alley and you have a 45-caliber automatic. However, it does not work very well if you are in the lobby of a brightly lit hotel where they are holding a police convention and 100 armed detectives are standing around chatting.

Force has an unfortunate history of success, but I firmly believe that influence and persuasion are infinitely more effective in the long run. People rarely change their minds when confronted with force, but they will fight to the death for something they believe in.

All good salespeople know their job is not to lead the horse to water and make it drink, but to make the horse thirsty. If you make your customers thirsty enough for your product or your service, you have a sale.

Never confuse force with power. If you have power, use it. Maximize your strengths and minimize your weaknesses. Be gentle, fair, and enthusiastic. This part of you is essential when you want to persuade others to your point of view. Tip O'Neill, former Speaker of the House, certainly had power and authority, but he preferred to persuade. He was a huge bear of a man, but never used his size or his authority to intimidate. He said, "You don't have to go to war to win the war." O'Neill and most effective sales communicators know that there are two kinds of power: position power and personal power.

POSITION POWER

Position power comes from the authority of the position you hold. You exercise this power because of the job you do or the title you have. Positions do influence, and it's very important not to waste position power. I've had some people working for me who were ashamed of being salespeople. If you asked them what they did for a living, they'd say, "Oh, I'm just a salesperson." Never downgrade your occupation. If you're not proud of it, don't do it. There are 35,000 job titles in the Government Statistical Abstract. Hopefully, there's at least one for which you are qualified and would be proud to do.

Position power is usually conferred by some force outside yourself. However, it can be implied by the image you project and the words you use. I don't mean you have to wear designer clothes or use only words that you've read in *Harvard Business Review*, but what you wear, your grooming, and how you carry yourself and express yourself are all part of a projecting a favorable image.

That goes for your actions, too. Although I happen to believe that Jimmy Carter was a reasonably good president and a splendid ex-president, I think he made a mistake when he told people, "Just call me Jimmy." To me, he was and will always be "Mr. President." There's the famous photograph of him carrying his own luggage while his entourage walks behind him with empty hands. Those images detracted from the importance of the presidency. On the other hand, Ronald Reagan understood the power of ceremony. Although he projected the image of being "just one of the guys," he never let anyone forget that he was one of the most powerful men in the world, the President of the United States. He had the power to reward and hand out "perks." He also had the power to coerce, to punish legislators who disagreed with him by instilling the fear that he could influence the public to vote against certain legislators at the next election. His position gave him power, and he used it.

The biggest problem with power derived solely from position is that it can vanish when you lose or leave your position. Any power that is awarded by others can be taken away just as easily. (Sometimes people who abuse their power of authority make a lot of enemies who are delighted to seek revenge once the abusers are no longer protected by that power.)

If you must choose whether to exert personal or position power, skip position power and use personality and persuasion. Think of the small but elite number of former political figures, sports stars, military heroes, and various public celebrities who maintain the esteem of the public long after their five minutes of fame have passed. That's the kind of power you want to have.

PERSONAL POWER

Personal power is who you are, what you know, and what values and philosophies guide your life. You project these attitudes to others through your self-confidence, self-esteem, and self-expression. These are skills, talents, and abilities that you consciously acquire all your life. The more you are and the more you know about who and what you are, the more power you will have to influence others.

One quality that guarantees personal power is *charisma*. It's a characteristic that is nearly impossible to define, one with mystical and magical overtones, but it's easy to identify. In a group, there's one person your eye is drawn to. In a crisis, there's one person everyone turns to. It's the ability to attract and influence others. Many think you have to be born with charisma, but I think it can be learned.

Charisma starts with having a dream, a vision, or a purpose that drives you. This purpose turns to a passion that is expressed in enthusiasm, sensitivity, and commitment. Add good communication skills to this passion, and you have a charismatic person.

YOUR SOURCES OF INFLUENCE

Influence involves a sender and a receiver. You are the sender and have control of how you present information. The receiver is your potential customer who controls his or her own receptivity. However, *you* control your ability to evaluate and assess that receptivity.

Therefore, your ability to persuade and influence depends on two factors:

1. How you send information
2. How you evaluate its reception and adjust future messages

Let's start with things you do that influence your customers and potential customers.

BE AN EXPERT

My father used to tell me that if you have a choice between doing business with a crook who knows what he's doing and an honest person who doesn't, choose the crook. You'll lose less money.

Actually, I don't think my father or anyone else would choose the crook, but the message is that customers want to do business with salespeople who know what they're doing. You can influence people when they believe you are an expert with the information, knowledge, and experience they need.

It's important to use your expertise in a persuasive manner. Never force it on anyone or be arrogant about it. Think of all those lawyer jokes. People ridicule what makes them uncomfortable, and many see lawyers as arrogant when they show off their legal expertise and academic credentials. You, as a good sales communicator, never want to seem arrogant, so use your expertise gently.

SHOW A CARING ATTITUDE

When you show concern for your customers and prove you are willing to serve them, they become receptive to you and your ideas. Remember the Hallmark slogan, "When you care enough to send the very best." Hallmark influenced our card-buying habits and became a multi-billion-dollar business.

Your personal confidence and friendliness help to establish a bond of trust. Of course, you can persuade in this manner through the mail or over the telephone, but you have more communication tools to work with when you present your ideas and products face to face.

Refer to "we" and "us." Do things *with* your customers, not *to* them. Include them, make them part of the solution. Your customers want someone on their side. Build the expectancy that you can help. Then deliver more than they expect, even more than you promised.

DEMONSTRATE SIMILAR BELIEFS
AND VALUES

We acquire influence when we convince others that we share or respect their beliefs, attitudes, and values. Relate your own values to the basic personal drives that shape others' decisions. In other words, sell what they have already bought.

Many years ago, a company hired me to train salespeople who sold recreational land. One of them was out-selling the other six salespeople on the team. I really wondered how he did it, so one Saturday I followed him around, not saying a word, just observing and listening. I noticed that he asked questions and then listened intently to the answers. When it came time to "sell," he basically ignored all of the facts and logic of the situation and appealed directly to the buyer's emotions. At one point he reached down, picked up a handful of dirt, put it under the customer's nose, and said, "Just smell that dirt. Have you smelled anything that fresh in years?" He talked about the clear skies, clean air, and green trees. That day he made three major sales. I never once heard him give any part of the company's recommended sales talk.

That evening over dinner, I asked him about his selling philosophy. He told me that the people who bought recreational land had already made the decision to buy when they were Boy Scouts or Camp Fire Girls. If they enjoyed their first camping trip, subconsciously they said, "Isn't this wonderful? Maybe someday I could live in a place like this." All he did was reawaken their dreams and show them how they could fulfill those dreams. He tapped into their beliefs, attitudes, and values. He sold them what they had already bought.

Some phrases that help you seek emotional agreement include:

- How would you feel?
- This is your moment.
- Haven't you waited long enough?
- With this product, you can be glamorous, classy, worldly, sophisticated, outrageous.
- Just try it. There now, how does that feel?
- You've done it!

KNOW YOUR CLIENTS

Before you can influence and persuade, you have to know your customer. Good sales communicators start by doing their homework. They research their potential clients to find out as much as possible about what will influence them to become customers.

What do you know about your customers' personalities? Do you know their beliefs, fears, hopes, behavior patterns, and business practices? Do you know what results they've gotten in the past and what their expectations are for the future?

What about their competition? Do you know what it is, how they feel about it, and what effect it has had on their businesses? Are you aware of other influences on their decisions, such as spouses, business partners, advisors, or friends? Often, a third party has enormous influence on a decision. Is this customer able to make a decision alone, or are other people's opinions important to him or her?

Any research you can do in advance is beneficial, but even face to face you can still learn things. Look at customers and their surroundings. What's on their desk? What clothes do they wear? What about their posture and energy level? Do they speak so fast it sounds like machine-gun fire, or are they thoughtful? Do they think aloud? We all listen from our own bias, but you should be asking yourself, "Who is this person who is talking to me?"

We can influence other people if we can discover their behavior patterns and react to them in a way that leads them to take action. Highly successful salespeople have learned to sell exactly the way the customer wants to buy.

They are persuasive because they connect with the customer's existing ideas, attitudes, and beliefs. Then, if necessary, they leverage and build on these attitudes and beliefs to introduce new ones. Everyone grows and changes. As a skilled communicator, you can be part of the process.

BE PERSISTENT

The power of persuasion usually exceeds the persuasion of power. Have you ever overheard a child in a supermarket?

"Mommy, I want some candy."

The mother says, "Not now, honey, it's too close to lunch."

A little later, you hear again, "Mommy, I want some candy."

Mommy says, "Not now, dear."

And isn't it funny how, when you get to the checkout counter, there's the child eating candy? Children are persistent. They know what they want. They ask for it, and they keep asking until they get it.

Salespeople can learn a lot by watching little children. They never took a class in overcoming objections or sales communication, but they are most persistent in stating what they want and creative in explaining why they should get it. Their endurance and enterprise are astonishing, and they can usually persuade the most reluctant adult.

Are you as persistent and creative as that? As salespeople, we have to come up with concepts, ideas, and solutions that other people can accept. Sometimes we have to persuade others to reframe their thought processes, to look at a situation from another perspective. We get them to ask, "Will this product or service really solve my problems, fix what's wrong, and help me?"

Tom Dashiell sells insurance and investment programs to small-business owners. One of his most successful products is a "cafeteria" benefits package for employees. That's a package that allows an employee to select from a large menu of health insurance, life insurance, annuities, various types of pension funds, payroll deduction savings, even child-care allowances. When he approaches prospects, their first question is about the monthly cost of offering these services to their employees. Their second question is, "Why should I do this?" Tom starts by agreeing that the benefits package is going to cost the company money. "But how much does it cost every time you lose an employee? Let's think about that. And all the costs involved in hiring and training a replacement. Turnover can cost you a great deal more than benefits for loyal employees. If you can keep your existing employees and motivate them to increase productivity, it's going to make your job a lot easier and you'll save money." Tom tells me that when he finds a business with high employee turnover, communicating this concept always leads to a sale.

TAKE RESPONSIBILITY

Not long ago, a woman called me to ask for my brochure and other information. She wanted to consider me as a speaker for a meeting she was having in the near future. I told her I was happy to receive her call and that I would mail her some information that very day — but under the pressure of several deadlines I forgot. Several days later, she called again to say she had not yet received my information, and that they were having a committee meeting the very next day to choose speakers. I apologized profusely and took full blame. I said I hoped she would give me another chance and asked what I could do to prove I really was a responsible person.

For a moment there was dead silence on the telephone. Then she said, "I am very impressed with your willingness to take total responsibility. Most of us try to blame other people or circumstances. Our audience needs to hear that very message about taking responsibility. If you can get your information to my committee by tomorrow morning, we will still consider you as our speaker." I offered to jump in my car, drive to her company, and hand-deliver the information. She said she was doubly impressed with that kind of service, and she looked forward to meeting me in person. I delivered. So did she. I got the job!

YOUR PERSUASION TECHNIQUES

"Influence" sometimes has a negative connotation. We hear about "influence peddling" and "undue influence." But influence is just the ability to show others that doing it your way has a lot of advantages. Isn't that what selling is? Influencing is always going on. Either you are influencing others or they are influencing you. The question is: Can you influence people to buy into your dreams, desires, and objectives? Influence is not changing someone's beliefs or actions by force. I believe it is impossible to change others unless they are willing to change. Otherwise, it's like trying to teach a gorilla to sing. It doesn't work, and it makes the gorilla really mad.

People must change themselves. You can't change them. All you can do is influence them to consider change. To do this, start by changing yourself. Change how you relate to a particular client or customer. Everyone is different, so you need a variety of skills and styles to relate to a certain individual at a particular moment about a particular issue. One memorized, rehearsed approach won't work. Successful communication is done issue by issue, moment by moment, and person by person. Only when you address all three facets can you influence the decision-making process.

When it comes to influencing people, there are two truths:

1. Everyone is different.
2. Everyone is the same.

People are very different—intellectually, spiritually, and emotionally—but at the most primary level everyone is the same. The same hope, fear, and excitement is in all of us. Emerson said, "To believe that what is true for you in your private heart is also true for all men—that is genius." What he was saying was that, deep down, all people feel the same. Each of us has experienced feelings of fear, weakness, helplessness, confusion, and uncertainty, as well as warmth, safety, and security. When you feel any of these things, you realize that others feel the same way.

Such feelings can be contagious. You can influence the feelings of others with your own, suggesting changes through your mood, words, and tone of voice. When you tap into your listeners' past experiences, you can elicit emotional responses that will influence their actions or behavior.

My wife Sheila and I had a day off while we were conducting some seminars in Australia, and we decided to take a sightseeing bus around Sydney. It was a warm day, and after touring a museum, we bought ice cream cones from a street vendor before returning to the bus. As we made our way to our seats, licking our cones, we passed a little boy, about four years old, with red hair and big blue eyes. He looked at our cones, then looked at his dad and said, "*I* like ice cream." There was no reaction from his father, so he repeated, "I *like* ice cream." Still no reaction. So he tried once more, "I like *ice cream.*" The father stared into his son's big blue eyes, saw the eagerness on his face, and heard the urgency in his voice. Then the man left the bus and returned with an ice cream cone.

This is a perfect example of using mood, words, and tone of voice to create empathy in someone else. To influence people, you have to touch them. This is what motivates. When you are in harmony with your customer's core emotions, you form a bond with him or her. Once that bond is established, you have an opportunity to influence his or her decisions.

10 INFLUENCING TECHNIQUES

Here are 10 specific strategies for persuading and influencing your customers.

1.   **Think small.** People rarely make big changes suddenly. Small changes are easier for most of us. If a panhandler asked you for $100, would you be likely to give it to him? Probably not. Yet, if you give the same panhandler only a quarter or two a day, you will soon have given away $100. In the same way, you can influence big decisions by making a series of smaller suggestions.

Be aware of the distance between a present attitude and a brand new idea. It is almost impossible to cause a major jump in people's minds, and be very wary if you do. A mind so easily changed can change back just as easily.

Big changes are best accomplished in small steps. Start by getting your prospects to accept an idea that is close to their old attitudes or beliefs. Then move them closer and closer to the new idea. Just remember that you can rarely bring about a major shift in the core values of a mentally healthy individual, nor should you try.

2.   **Stimulate identification.** There are some people we respect and want to be like. There are others we envy and want to imitate. Whether the desire to emulate has high or low motives, it's a useful selling tool: "Your neighbors just purchased our new landscape program to keep their property beautiful. Would you like your grounds to be as handsome as theirs are?"

This is a very common advertising technique. Sports figures, pop stars, and cultural icons endorse every product, service, and charitable cause known to humanity, and "keeping up with the Joneses" is a traditional neighborhood pastime. Your job is to identify whose opinion your prospect truly values and then personalize your appeal.

3. Use the positive/negative approach. This is the classic carrot/stick approach of donkey drivers. You lure the donkey forward with something desirable (the carrot) while offering negative consequences for hanging back (the stick).

Show both the good your product can do and the bad things that may happen if it isn't used. A good exercise is to make two lists. At the top of the first sheet, write "Positive" and list all the benefits of your product or service, such as how great it is, how well it performs, and what fantastic results it offers. At the bottom, write a statement about what and how you can guarantee these results.

On the second sheet, write "Negative," and list everything negative that could happen if the customer doesn't use the product. At the bottom of this second page, write a statement of how you can help the customer avoid these horrible consequences.

As you talk to your customers, balance the positive and negative. Point ahead to a rosy picture of life with the product, then point back toward the bleak and unproductive events that await the unwary who fail to use it. Alternate the carrot and the stick, gently moving the customer forward.

4. Appeal to Logic and Emotion. Remember my formula, L +R+E=S (Logic plus Reason plus Emotion equals Success). All decisions include an element of self-fulfillment. The professional salesperson cannot afford to ignore the emotional factors in persuasion. Logic and reason ride on the back of emotion. Customers decide to buy or not buy for emotional reasons, but they back up their decisions with logic and reason.

To appeal to both emotion and logic, appeal to both the left half and the right half of the customer's brain. There is a sound biological reason why the decision process is divided between the left brain (logic) and right brain (emotion). Each of the human brain's spheres or sides control different processes. The left side is the logical, verbal side that sorts facts and figures. The right side is the emotional, visual, spatial side. This right half is good at organizing by size, shape, and distance. It provides the intuitive power necessary to assign values and relationships to all of the facts and figures that are perceived by the left side of the brain. Everyone uses both sides of their brain, adjusting the balance to the task at hand.

Some people are noticeably better at using numbers or at doing a job that requires strong spatial skills. One half of their brain is dominant most of the time. When you are questioning or making a statement to a prospect or customer, decide whether the logical left brain or the emotional right brain seems to be dominant and adjust your presentation so that it is either more logical or more emotional.

For example, your customer wants to know what something costs. That sounds simple, but is it the right or the left brain that's asking? If it's a left-brain request for numbers, offer price comparisons, statistics, return on investment, start-up costs, and operating costs. But if the right brain is saying, "I don't know if I can afford this. I'm uncomfortable. Do I want to commit to this cost in view of all the other expenses I have?" then tie the purchase to a larger vision. Create a picture of the final result. Relieve discomfort by stressing that maybe a payment plan combined with increased productivity would actually reduce costs.

To check whether you're dealing with right-brain or left-brain concerns, you might ask questions like these:

Your Question:
Is the immediate cost the most important factor in your decision, or are you more concerned with the long-term value?

Prospect's Left-Brain Response:	*Prospect's Right-Brain Response:*
Tell me the immediate cost.	*"What is the long term value?*

Your Question:
Are you concerned this might not be the right step for you now?

Prospect's Left-Brain Response:	*Prospect's Right-Brain Response:*
Give me the figures and I'll decide for myself.	*I'm not sure how this fits in with all the other things I'm doing.*

Watch for clues so you don't dump a lot of statistics on a prospect who is in an intuitive, right-brain mode, or stress the relationships of your products to the long-term aspirations of a prospect who is operating from the fact-finding left brain. Influence by being in harmony with the half of the customer's brain that is currently dominant.

Good sales communicators touch both sides of the brain. When you list the logical benefits for a customer and then frame those benefits in terms that touch emotions, you will be very persuasive. Appeal to the whole brain, but emphasize your message to the side that you think is the primary information processor at that particular moment. When you merge them, your customer understands in a way that brings vividness, credibility, and depth to the factual reality. The product of imagination without thought or the product of thought without imagination leaves a vacuum in understanding.

Here's an example of using logic and emotion. An army sergeant in World War II persuaded every soldier in his company to buy a $10,000 government life insurance policy. How did he do it? He told them there was a good chance they would be sent overseas to fight and that the government was offering this insurance at a very low monthly premium. If they were killed, the government was going to send their families $10,000. Although that would not replace them in the hearts of their loved ones, it would go a long way toward helping their families financially. On the other hand, he told them, if they didn't buy the insurance and got killed overseas, the government was not going to send their families a penny. Then he asked his emotional closing question: "Who do you think the government is going to send to the front line first? The ones that cost the government $10,000 or the ones that won't cost anything?" That sergeant may not have thought of himself as a salesperson, but he certainly used the elements of logic and emotion to close his sale.

The perfect phrase is one that appeals simultaneously to logic and emotion. When you understand what motivates your prospect, a few words may be sufficient. A mutual fund salesperson I know uses the slogan: "Invest in stocks now, make money soon, lie on the beach forever." In those few words he has appealed to both logic and emotion.

5. Appeal to the five motivations. Remember the five motivators we talked about in Step One—profit, peace of mind, pleasure, pain, and pride? You can design persuasive phrases for each of these motivators that appeal to both logic and emotion. Here are some examples to start your thinking.

Profit. Everyone wants to get ahead or at least stay even. Fear of loss is the mirror image of profit and sometimes an even more powerful motivator.

- Are you throwing your money away on a rent check?
- This car will save you more than $50,000 over the next 10 years.
- Can you think of a better investment?
- How safe is your money? With this plan, you'll never lose a dime. The U.S. government guarantees it.

Peace of mind. This means freedom from stress and fear, something everyone seeks from infancy. It is a primal urge.

- Do you want to keep on top of what's going on in your industry?
- Are you ever embarrassed by ... ? Never again!
- You'll never run out of gas again!
- This will last you 30 years.

Pleasure. People can derive pleasure from just about anything, even discomfort. ("No pain, no gain" or "If it itches, you know it's healing.") Life is a constant succession of small pleasures. As the song says, "the best things in life are free," but even free pleasures can be enhanced and amplified by a skilled salesperson.

- See the full moon over Mauna Loa from the deck of this romantic cruise ship.
- Imagine your garden banked with gorgeous blooms.
- Isn't it time to treat yourself to … ?
- We cater to your every whim.
- Don't you deserve … ?
- This will be the most fun you've ever had.

Pain. Physical and emotional pain is something most of us want to avoid. Most of us know what we can do to avoid pain caused by poor diet, poor health habits, overindulgence, or neglect, but for some it seems like too much trouble until the pain starts. The ethical salesperson motivates prospects to care for themselves and their environment by balancing fear of pain with appeals to pride, pleasure, and peace of mind.

- Remember the last time you were in the dentist's chair? How would you like to make your next trip a pleasure?
- Stop headaches before they start!
- Lower-back pain is a pain in the … lower back! Stand tall with …
- Did you freeze last winter? This will keep you warm and toasty …
- Happy feet aren't an accident. End painful corns, calluses, and bunions by …

Pride. A customer who is driven by the positive aspects of pride (self-esteem, achievement, a sense of accomplishment) can be persuaded by appealing to the desire to be thought of as a capable person. Use phrases that appeal to self-expression, self-esteem, self-confidence, self-worth, self-mastery, and self-image.

- Our product unleashes your creativity.
- Our service gives you a clear advantage.
- This gives you a competitive edge.
- You'll have skills you can use all your life.

What phrases would you use to appeal to each of the motivators? The more you can combine logic, reason, and emotion, the better your chance of influencing your buyer.

6. Never argue. If you want to persuade, never argue. Never defend your position, no matter how strong it is. If you become defensive or argumentative, you may win the battle, but you will lose the war. I've actually seen childish debates between a salesperson and a customer about who was right and who was wrong.

Whenever you want to persuade, first agree with *whatever* your clients say. Then use that agreement to direct their attention to another point of view. "Yes, you're absolutely right. Most people prefer that method, so I was really surprised when I saw how it performed under these different conditions. Do any of them apply to you?"

Protect their self-image. In Asia, they call this "saving face." Lead your customers through an analysis of their position and the benefits you can offer. Always be polite in your language and tone. Treat all prospects with great kindness and concern.

Your job is to persuade people to do what they ought to do if there were no persuasion. "This is good for you." "I have your best interests at heart." "Trust me." Of course, you don't use those exact words, but that's what you convey when you're trying to persuade. Offer reasons, examples, or references so buyers don't have to take your word for it. Your aim is a mutually beneficial conclusion.

7.   **Overcome resistance.** When you meet resistance, rejoice. All your influencing skills are going to get a workout. The following list shows persuasive approaches to overcoming some common objections.

"I'm not interested." Many people say that before they even know what you're selling. If you can discover why, you can persuade by emphasizing the benefits that your product or service would bring them. For example:

Prospect: *I'm just not interested in putting in storm windows.*

Salesperson: *Of course not. Who wants storm windows? What most of us want is to keep the heat in the house so we're more comfortable and save money on energy. Is there any reason why you wouldn't want to be comfortable if it didn't cost you any more than what you're spending now on gas and electric bills?*

"We're perfectly happy with our current supplier." People resist doing things differently—even if they know they are wrong—because what they've been doing is usually more comfortable. To overcome this inertia, show how change will produce greater comfort and rewards. Begin by establishing what the buyer is getting now and then move on to how you can give more. Your approach might go like this:

> *I can understand your present satisfaction. You're dealing with a very good firm. Maybe you would be willing to tell me what it is about your present supplier that makes you happy.*
>
> *Those are great reasons. Let me ask you another question. Have you ever had any problems with your supplier? The reason I ask is that our cus-*

tomers are constantly telling us how much they appreciate …

Then list your benefits. This is particularly effective if you can concentrate on any weakness your competitor has. But never disparage the competitor, and never argue with the customer. Simply suggest that there is a better way.

"Gee, I'm sorry. I buy everything from a friend of mine." Your formula for persuading this individual is to agree, then ask questions and confirm. You could ask, "What do you like most about the service your friend gives you?" Listen attentively. Then ask something like, "Why don't you tell me exactly what I would have to do to become your business friend and receive at least a small part of your purchase orders?" You may only get your foot in the door, but over time you will have an opportunity to use further persuasion.

"We're doing fine just like we are." Compliment this buyer on his or her success and try to up-sell him or her into purchasing additional products or new, improved models. You do this by asking, "Did you know that we just added four new, improved models to our line?" or "We've made a lot of improvements and additions to our product line that I think would really benefit your company," or "Did you see the new product announcement that we made in all the trade newspapers? We're now the talk of the industry." Once you have introduced the concept, you ask a question like, "Would you rather come to our show-room to take a look at the new models, or shall I bring some by?" or "When can I show you this new process in action?" or "One of our clients has come up with a unique way to use this product, and they say it saves them a bundle. Would you like to know how?"

When customers recognize what is good for them, what they want, and how to obtain it, they literally sell themselves. All you do is take the order or ring up the sale. But in most cases customers only recognize that they are dissatisfied with the way things are now. They are also suspicious of any solution that a salesperson suggests. They suspect, quite accurately, that the salesperson has a financial interest in the outcome of the exchange. To pretend otherwise is pure hypocrisy on your part, but acknowledging the commercial aspects of the exchange doesn't have to lessen your position as a skilled advisor.

8. Build on past experiences. Another way to persuade is to tap into the past, to invoke nostalgia. Identify pleasant memories and tie them to future expectations, suggesting that customers can experience them again with your product. For example, my wife Sheila and I bought a Cadillac back in 1977 and drove it for 13 years. We put over 150,000 miles on it and, except for normal servicing, new tires, and new brakes, the car never needed repair. We liked the looks of it. We liked the service it gave us. We liked the comfort of the ride. Are we sold on Cadillacs? You bet. So when it was time to trade that car in, a salesperson who knew our past history could very easily have used our past experience to sell us a new Cadillac. We would have been easy to persuade.

However, we ran into a Jaguar salesperson who was skilled at the "A lot of people feel that way … " approach. This is where you validate something that people already believe to be true because of their past experience, then suggest they consider another possibility, gently leading them through questions and provocative statements to accept the change. That's the process we went through, and we bought a Jaguar instead of another Cadillac.

We already believed that the Jaguar was a top-of-the-line automobile and equal to the Cadillac in performance. I thought the looks of the Jaguar were superior to the Cadillac. The suggestion was that we would be just as happy as we had been with the Cadillac. Emotionally the Jaguar offered extra pleasure, and intellectually it seemed like a good deal since it wouldn't lose its resale value. The only question left for us to answer was, "Would you like to give it a try?" The salesperson tapped into our beliefs, built on past experiences, suggested considering a different possibility, and then used a series of questions and statements to lead us to accept a change.

That's how persuasion works. It's telling a believable story and creating a compelling reason for a different action by creating a new image in the customer's mind. If you are perceived as honest, trustworthy, and credible, you can "futurize," building mental pictures of your product or service benefiting your customer. Bring the future into the present. Other examples of building on past experiences include:

Remember the homemade bread your mother used to make? The smell of it when you came in the front door? The taste when you covered it with butter and jam? The crispy crust? How'd you like to experience that again? The MasterBaker Bread machine lets you make two loaves of wholesome, nourishing bread without endless kneading and standing around the kitchen waiting for the dough to rise. Just pop in the ingredients and come back to perfect bread.

Can't you just see yourself, lying on the beach with someone waving a palm frond over you to keep you cool while someone else brings you a tall Piña Colada? That's what might happen if you buy a lottery ticket today."

The future image, tied to the product, persuades people to buy. Find an area of agreement and then futurize by building a picture of how it can be. But remember that life is not a win-lose contest. To succeed, get in sync with your customers' beliefs, perceptions, and feelings. Then move with them, not against them.

I learned this lesson when my young sons, Bill and Tom, were taking judo lessons. I would sit on the sidelines and watch the class practice every Saturday. Their teacher, Mr. Higashi, would say over and over again, "Use the strength of the other person. Go with the flow."

Effective salespeople go with the flow too. I went into a hardware store the other day to buy a nine-volt battery. All the batteries were prepackaged in plastic with either two or four to a pack. When I explained to the clerk that I only needed and wanted one battery, she went into her "salesperson mode."

First she told me she would be happy to open the package and sell me just one battery. Then she explained that she would have to charge me a little bit extra because there was a special discount on purchasing two. She told me that the batteries had an 18-month shelf life. She suggested that it might be a good idea to buy the package of two, get the discounted price, and have a spare so I wouldn't have to make a special trip to purchase another one. There's nothing worse than finding a dead battery at an inconvenient time. I conceded that she had convinced me. She could sell me two batteries.

"But don't you think it's an even better idea to buy the

pack of four?" This woman was a great salesperson. She totally agreed that I could purchase one battery if that was what I really wanted. That's going with the flow. Then she futurized a picture of what life would be like if my one battery went dead. And finally she suggested an alternative choice: Buy the pack!

Thomas Jefferson said that in matters of principle, we should stand firm like a rock, but in matters of opinion we should flow like a river. When you are trying to persuade your customers to your point of view, meet them at their present position and suggest new directions. Reinforce existing attitudes first. People do not like change and resist new messages that don't fit their current beliefs. To persuade, first agree and then suggest. What we're trying to do is to change the other person's attitude before we change his or her actions.

Ask yourself what will change this other person's attitude. Remember that the change you're going for, through persuasion, is only a temporary change. You're not trying to change core beliefs, simply get agreement for the moment.

9. Use emotional triggers. Most people are influenced by unconscious triggers. Their experiences make them respond to catalysts of which they're not even aware. When we are babies, we learn to cry to get food or dry diapers. That response stays with us throughout our life. We know that crying will usually cause a response in others. Certain words and the way in which they are delivered also trigger behavior reactions.

Yale University researchers came up with a list of the 12 most persuasive words:

discovery	new
easy	proven
guarantee	results
health	safety
love	save
money	you

Here are some examples of phrases using these words:

- You're guaranteed proven results.
- This new discovery makes it easy!
- Saves you money!
- You care about the health and safety of those you love.

Using the right words can create an atmosphere of acceptance, trust, and respect.

10. Identify perceived needs. In my seminars, I ask participants to analyze their own personal motivations by giving a value to 14 basic human needs. Maybe you would like to do the same. Rate each need from 1, the most important, to 14, the least important.

_____	Independence
_____	Good health
_____	Acceptance
_____	Affection
_____	Wealth
_____	Self-respect
_____	Accomplishment

_____	Power
_____	Status
_____	Spiritual wholeness
_____	Self-expression
_____	Recognition
_____	Fun
_____	Security

Now that you have gained some personal insights, you are better equipped to evaluate how customers would rate these factors. Does having fun overcome any need for security or status? Is independence more important than affection or power more important than acceptance? Make an educated guess, then watch for clues that confirm or disprove your guess. It is human nature for people to say they want one thing but then choose another. Consider the following dialogues.

You: _How important are safety features?_

Prospect: _Oh, very important. Does that come in red? (Clue: The prospect is probably more interested in status, self-expression, or fun.)_

You: _This is one of our most popular models._

Prospect: _Glances briefly, then looks elsewhere. (Clue: Status and acceptance are not high priorities.)_

You: _The ecologically friendly model is more expensive._

Prospect: _How does it help the environment? (Clue: Appeal to self-respect and spiritual wholeness.)_

You: _The ecologically friendly model is more expensive._

Prospect: _(making a slight face) How much is this one over here? (Clue: Appeal to recognition, status, power, fun, or another need relevant to the product.)_

You:　　　*The ecologically friendly model is more expensive.*

Prospect:　　*How much more expensive? (Clue: Prospect is weighing self-interest versus selflessness. Wait for more clues.)*

When you identify your prospects' real motivations, you are better equipped to persuade.

WHEN PASSION ISN'T ENOUGH

You may believe in something totally and still not be able to persuade others to share in that belief. Winston Churchill and Lady Astor belonged to opposing political parties and were legendary for their arguments. Once Lady Astor turned to Winston Churchill and said, "Mr. Churchill, if you were my husband, I would put poison in your coffee." Churchill replied, "Lady Astor, if I were your husband, I'd drink it!"

Obviously they both felt strongly about their positions, but they didn't establish the bond necessary to influence and persuade. Influencing is the skill of getting someone do something without using force, coercion, or the authority of your position.

You persuade when you see, feel, and listen as the other person, sending messages like:

- We are alike.
- I'm on your side.
- You see things my way.
- I see your point.
- I feel good about your suggestions.

That is influencing.

PERSUASION VERSUS COERCION

Red Motley, the famous salesman and writer, said, "Nothing happens until someone sells a product, a service, or an idea." I agree, but I also believe there is a flip side to persuasion and influencing. If we callously manipulate people, if we try to deceive them or coerce them, we are not dealing in an ethical way that benefits either our customers or ourselves.

So my definition of persuasion is "suggestion." The real goal of persuasion is to get the best possible outcome for all participants in the transaction—a win-win situation. To achieve this, we must be totally open and honest in sharing information. We must care about the other person's welfare and sincerely believe our solution is the right one. Then we must offer a choice. High pressure may make a sale, but it destroys the sales relationship and any possibility of future business. No truly professional salesperson will sacrifice future growth for temporary gain.

STEP SEVEN

NEGOTIATE (HOW DO YOU GET WHAT YOU WANT?)

My friend Roger Dawson, an internationally known speaker and author of the book, Secrets of Power Negotiating, *tells about the day his kitchen flooded. A plumber arrived and offered to fix the problem for $50. Roger agreed. Two minutes later the problem was solved and the plumber asked for his money.*

> Roger said, "Fifty dollars for two minutes work? I'm an internationally known speaker and I don't make that kind of money!"
>
> The plumber smiled. "Neither did I when I was an internationally known speaker."

There are three important points in this story. First, often money is not the main issue in negotiation. When you have an urgent need, then any price becomes acceptable as long as you can afford it. Second, once services have been performed and emergencies taken care of, the value of the service diminishes sharply in the buyer's mind. And third, the outcome of any negotiation depends on the balance of power between the parties.

This is certainly true in selling. Prospects start with the power to buy or not to buy. But sometimes prospects have a need, and the salesperson has the ability to fill it. The balance of power then shifts to the salesperson. Sales negotiations must recognize the strengths and weaknesses of both the customer and the salesperson. Even when the greater strength of one party influences the outcome of negotiation, the real goal should be to work out the situation to the advantage of both parties.

Negotiation is the art of the possible, the ability to make a deal, the skill of getting agreement. In almost every sales transaction, a certain amount of negotiation has to take place. Roger Dawson, in his book *Secrets of Power Negotiating,* divides negotiations into three steps:

1. Clarify the objective. Know what you want and find out what the other person wants.

2. Gather information about the other person. Find out who they are, what is important to them, and why.

3. Get agreement and obtain mutual satisfaction. Sometimes this is accomplished through compromise.

Negotiation doesn't always involve price. It can include give-and-take on any aspect of the sales process. You want something, or the other person wants something. Which of you should win? Both! That's not always easy, but it's possible if you have a clear idea about what you want.

1. Describe what you really want in one sentence.

2. Find out what the other person really wants; never assume you know. Do research, make an educated guess, and then do the most obvious thing: Ask! Just be sure you are asking the right person. Ask in a way that gets a thoughtful response. Now, describe what the customer really wants.

3. Ask yourself what you can give each other in return for what you want. Ask and keep asking. In negotiation, people have only four choices:
   - To accept the situation as it is
   - To leave and get nothing
   - To change their own desires
   - To change the other person's viewpoint, desires, or wants

WHY NEGOTIATE?

Trading, bargaining, bartering, haggling, and dealing all have an ancient and honorable tradition in most (but not all) cultures. Some people can't enjoy anything unless they feel they have taken advantage of the seller and gotten a deal. Others consider it downright rude to ask for a lower price. They assume that the seller is already offering the lowest possible price and to question it would be to insult his or her integrity. Buying, for these people, is strictly a take-it-or-leave-it proposition.

Of course, in some situations it is impossible to bargain. (Imagine asking a toll collector on a busy bridge to lower the 75-cent fee while honking cars pile up behind you.) Lots of prices today are set and are not subject to change. Since the Industrial Revolution in the last century, it is often possible to establish production costs to within a fraction of a cent. Efficient work methods and regulated wages can also fix labor costs. And sometimes mandated price controls legislate how much a dealer can charge.

So, why do we still need to know how to negotiate? Because all social exchanges—in everything from love and trust to goods and services—involve two parties' differing needs and wants. Until those needs and wants are defined and aligned, the transaction can't be completed satisfactorily. Nations negotiate treaties; businesses negotiate contracts; employees negotiate pay raises; children negotiate bedtimes and how much TV they can watch. Negotiation is a given of our civilization.

Sometimes the participants see these negotiations as a confrontation, a sort of battle in which the winner conquers and vanquishes the loser. I believe that a more productive approach is one of conciliation and compromise, a process that makes both participants winners.

WIN-WIN NEGOTIATIONS

Win-win negotiations are based on trust, understanding, respect, and ethics. Ethics means doing the right thing in the right way at the right time, and never taking unfair advantage. That is a real win-win negotiation.

You start by separating the problem from the people. Then you solve the problem without blaming or criticizing. Throughout, you treat your prospects and customers with a great deal of respect, trying to understand their points of view.

Yes, there are some salespeople who equate winning with conquering. They are obsessed with dominating and overpowering the other person. I believe that real winning means we consider the other person's needs throughout the transaction. It is a moral obligation as well as an intelligent business practice to see that our customers are not taken advantage of and that they win by achieving their needs or having their problems solved.

The late sports mediator Bob Wolf said, "You don't have to be disagreeable to disagree." Every good negotiator knows this is true. There is room in the world for people of good will to have different opinions, desires, and needs. But you can always connect with your customers when they believe you have their best interests at heart.

ONE WIN-WIN SUCCESS

Most buyers think used-car salespeople are at the bottom of the food chain when it comes to integrity and ethics. When someone offers us a car that belonged to an elderly schoolteacher who only drove it once a week to church, most of us grab our wallets and hang on.

But I have a personal story about a used-car salesman named Nick Peccarro. The name of Nick's business was Value Autos. In my opinion, Nick gave value. Some years ago, I was buying a used automobile for my 16-year-old daughter. Of course, she wanted the flashiest car on Nick's lot. Nick asked why she wanted the flashy one, and she said that she would be the youngest girl in her high school with her own car, and she wanted to be noticed.

Nick said, "I think I have a better automobile for you that will still accomplish your purpose." He showed her a plain, sturdy little Volkswagen Bug painted light blue.

Nick told me that he knew the previous owner of this automobile. Though it had a lot of miles on it, it had never been in an accident, and Nick's mechanic had totally reconditioned it. Now it was in top shape with brand new tires.

Then he turned to my daughter. The expression on her face showed she didn't think much of it. Nick said, "What if our sign painter decorates this car with a big rainbow on each side and across the back? We could use four or five bright colors and you'd certainly be noticed." My daughter began to show some enthusiasm. "But it doesn't have a radio," she said. I added that I thought the price was a little high for the year and the make. Nick said, "With the work that we've done to put this car in top condition, I really have to get this price. But, I'll tell you what I can do. Since your daughter wants a radio, I will have a good radio installed and paint the rainbows on the car without any extra charge."

Ending right here would be a good sales story of integrity selling, but Nick went even further. He called my daughter once a month for the next three months to ask her if she was still happy with the car or if she had any problems. Once or twice there were minor things wrong. Each time he said, "Bring it in tomorrow, and I'll fix that without charge." At the end of the third month, Nick showed up at our front door with his mechanic. He told my daughter that he would like to take a test drive in the car and have his mechanic check it out and service it, just to be sure that everything was okay.

Did we all win in that sales negotiation? We sure did! My daughter Julie got a car that made her feel important because the other students gave her lots of attention. The car ran almost perfectly and got great mileage. I paid the full price, but I felt good because Julie got the paint job, the radio, and extraordinary service without charge. Nick also won because my referrals have been responsible for at least a dozen people buying used cars from him.

INVISIBLE NEGOTIATING

My belief is that professional salespeople often know more about what is good for a client than the client does. Therefore, the client benefits from the salesperson's persuasion and negotiation skills.

One of the secrets of good negotiation is that the customer should never know you are negotiating. Negotiation should seem like a natural, comfortable process that is not forced. Concentrate on making your prospects or customers comfortable, taking away their anxieties, concerns, and fears. Focus on getting in sync with their current intellectual and emotional needs.

Never present a take-it-or-leave-it situation. Help them save face if they have previously taken a stand that cannot be reconciled with the current reality. Don't let them feel they are backing down. You can do this with carefully planned phrases.

- I hope you can understand this is my best offer.
- This is the very best I can do. Would you consider this offer?
- If you are willing to give up some part of the service, I can accept your price. Is that an option for you?

This particular technique was especially useful to me recently. In a training program proposal to a prospective client, I had agreed to do a full day of research on the organization so I could tailor my remarks to the company's exact needs and provide each participant with a customized workbook at the seminars. In addition, each member of the audience would get a free copy of my book *Questions That Make the Sale*. The vice president of sales accepted the proposal with one change. He wanted me to lower my fee by 20 percent.

Our conversation indicated that the vice president simply liked to feel he was getting a deal. The 20-percent price reduction made him feel good, as if he had won in the negotiation. I countered by saying I'd accept his price if I was not required to give free books. Instead, I would offer them for sale in the back of the room. And since I had audio tapes on the same subject, perhaps I could also offer them. This allowed my prospect to get the 20-percent reduction, which made him very happy, and it allowed me to sell products to the 150 participants, which actually increased my gross revenue for the event. This was a real win-win negotiation, and everybody was happy with the solution. We avoided the negotiation deadlock that comes when one party says, "This is my final offer — take it or leave it." Each of us was willing to make a concession to avoid deadlock.

SIX NEGOTIATION DO'S AND DON'TS

Over the years, I've learned a lot of basic do's and don'ts in negotiating. They can be summed up like this:

1. **Do your homework.** Know market conditions and market prices so you won't get drawn into a bidding war with your competition. Know your potential customers, what they need, how they will use your product or service, how it can benefit them, and what alternatives they have. And know every factor affecting the prices you can offer without hurting your own company.

2. **Don't negotiate with nondecision makers.** Early in the sales process, ask, "Is there anyone besides you who will be involved in making the final decision?" or "If we worked out an agreement that is comfortable for you, would you be prepared to complete the paperwork today?"

3. **Justify your price.** The price is always too high if purchasers don't perceive value for their money. What will this purchase do to increase productivity, reduce stress, improve daily operations, or increase profits? Justify your price! Show how ultimate cost, including longevity of use and lower maintenance, will offset any extra initial cost. And remember that fear of loss is a strong motivator, so emphasize the disadvantages of *not* buying as well as the benefits of accepting your offer.

4. **Offer extra value for the price.** If your customer still asks for a price reduction, offer him or her something extra, such as a service

contract, consultation time to solve a particular problem, or a free maintenance check after three months. Give something extra to create more value for the price asked.

5. **Offer a lower price for less value.** In exchange for a price reduction, ask your customers to take less or give you more. Reduce the price if they will agree to pay more quickly or to purchase additional quantities of the same product or a related product. Or say, "If you'll agree to give up the service contract, we can drop the price." Another possibility is, "If you pick up your order at our warehouse, we can knock off the delivery charges."

6. **Don't forget you are giving away your company's profits.** Every dollar that you take off the price and every extra service you provide comes off the profits of the company and your sales commissions. If the company doesn't make a profit, they will go out of business. That's not good for the customer or you.

BE WILLING TO WALK AWAY

Learn how to communicate the concessions you are willing to make to negotiate the sale. In other words, know your limits. How much can you give away? When will you walk away? Although it is important to reach a mutual agreement, you have to be willing to lose or you'll never win.

Always be willing to walk away, but don't give up so easily that you end up buying back your product. I've seen many salespeople go through the entire sales process, then refuse to negotiate some small point at the end and lose the sale.

My wife and I were in Monterey, California, walking through Cannery Row. She saw a beautiful water fountain that she thought would be ideal for our backyard. It was very expensive. Using her very best negotiating skills, she asked the owner of the store if he could do better on the price. He said no, the price was firm.

She said, "I'll tell you what. If you throw in the sales tax and the shipping to our home in Burlingame, 70 miles from here, we'll buy it right now and give you a check."

He said, "No, my price is my price. You have to pay sales tax and shipping yourself."

He was willing to lose, and he did. We decided that we could find another equally attractive fountain somewhere else.

A WIN-WIN STORY

A meeting planner recently asked me to do a three-hour training program at her company's convention but pleaded that her budget wouldn't cover my usual fee. I offered to add value for the price, that is, I'd deliver a keynote speech to open the conference at no additional charge. She quickly accepted, using the money allocated for a keynote speaker to make up my regular price. Since I was going to be at the convention anyway, and since I have given hundreds of keynote speeches, it was not a major concession for me to add an extra talk as part of the package. And it was an extra win for her because she had to pay transportation costs for only one speaker instead of two.

RECOGNIZING PERSONALITY TYPES

You will be dealing with lots of different people. Everyone is not the same. We encounter at least four basic personality types. Knowing how they operate can give you a negotiating advantage.

1. **Friendly and pleasant.** These people are generally energetic, confident, and clear about their goals. When you deal with these people, be personal, real, and agreeable. Show how your opinions and ideas match theirs.

2. **Shy and quiet.** These people are often very sensitive. They require and desire privacy. With this type, you can't be blunt or straightforward. Be tactful, polite, and patient, but don't try to be too personal because you'll scare these people away.

3. **Curt and gruff.** Some surly types are softies who fear being taken advantage of so they have developed a defensive front. Others are shy, stressed, busy, or just plain unpleasant people. Whatever the reason, don't react to their abruptness. Take a deep breath, lower your voice, and smile. Ask as many questions as they'll allow to draw them out. Keep them talking, and use their names. Agree with their points, and ask them to help you.

4. **Noncommittal.** These people are the toughest and most frustrating types to deal with. They agree with everything or nothing. Your goal is to get them involved in the process—physically and intellectually—as soon and as deeply as possible. For example, to involve people physically, hand them something or get them to do

something. Get them to sit in a car and start the motor, try on a garment, or sort photos of different models into "like" and "dislike" piles. To involve people intellectually, ask, "Could you tell me what you already know about this service? It will save us time."

Whether these customers are just being polite, have no sales resistance, or are unable to make a decision, involving them breaks down their resistance and makes them participants in the negotiation.

Many of these personality traits can and do overlap, but by defining them, we increase our ability to negotiate from a strong position. Of course, there are always crossover areas when trying to fit complex humans into a few simple categories. Some prospects will switch from one attitude to another right in the middle of the sales process. For example, an overly friendly approach may turn Ms. Shy-and-Quiet into Ms. Curt-and-Gruff, whereas a lighter one can result in Ms. Pleasant-and-Friendly. Be ready to switch gears and keep going.

By showing enthusiasm and genuine interest, you can sometimes switch people to another personality type. Dr. James Penton, whose job is to provide technical support for one of the top U.S. scientific instrument manufacturers, often accompanies salespeople on calls. He told me about the time he and a salesperson called on the purchasing manager at Rockwell Space Shuttle Station in Palmdale, California. The purchasing manager was very abrupt. He saw about 20 salespeople a day, and his manner was, "Get in, give your story, and get out." It was obvious that he was in a hurry, so the sales interview had to be brief.

However, Dr. Penton has been an avid space buff since he was a small child. He said that if there was any way he could look around the assembly building and actually touch a space shuttle, it would be the thrill of a lifetime. Suddenly the purchasing manager went from Mr. Curt-and-Gruff to Mr. Pleasant-and-Friendly. He, too, was a space buff and excited about the Palmdale operation. Forgetting his stress and tight schedule, he took Dr. Penton on a tour.

Unfortunately, the poor salesperson was completely forgotten and had to trail along behind them. Fortunately, when the tour was over, the purchasing manager made an appointment to see the salesperson the next day. So, be ready to adapt your style and words to deal with people on their terms.

SEVEN NEGOTIATING TECHNIQUES

To be really successful, negotiation must produce a win-win outcome. You are as valuable to the customer as the customer is to you. Negotiation can be regarded as a game of strategies and tactics. Even (or especially) if the prospective customer regards you as an opponent to be vanquished, you need to keep the playing field level so the outcome is mutually advantageous. Here are seven negotiating techniques to fall back on with overly demanding customers.

1. **How's that again?** Adopt this posture when someone introduces excessive demands into the negotiation process. Don't get excited or upset. Don't fight back. Instead, adopt a neutral demeanor. You want to seem tentative. Play dumb, saying things like, "I don't under-

stand. What price did you say?" or "I don't know about this. What do you think?" or "But we've already confirmed those points, haven't we? Shall we go over them again?" Seem mildly surprised but never irritated.

2. "Take away options" routine. Also called the "if you can qualify" negotiation technique. Life insurance salespeople use it all the time, but it can work in other situations. A life insurance salesperson says something like, "If you can qualify, I will let you buy $10 billion worth of insurance. But first we must find out about your health, income, and habits." The idea is that you're not going to sell just because someone has the money. There are other factors, and prospects must convince sellers they deserve to be allowed to buy. It's like having to take Political Science 101 before being allowed into an advanced class. This switches the balance from the prospect, who *may* be willing to buy, to you, who *may* be willing to sell.

3. Appeal to a higher authority. "Someone else must okay this." That's the TO (take over) or "second voice" technique often used by car dealers. "Well, it looks to me like it's a good deal, but before we can finalize it, I have to get the okay from my sales manager." In general selling, the TO means you refer tough questions or resistant prospects to an expert within your company or another salesperson who will back you up or offer another point of view.

4. Set-aside technique. This is a variation of TO: "I don't know if the boss would approve that price. But let's just set that aside for the moment and see if we can agree on these other points first." Whatever the prospects object to, delay addressing the objection and continue to check off points of agreement.

5. **Back-down margin maneuver.** Leave yourself enough margin for negotiation so you can back down. Don't start out so close to your bottom price that there is nowhere to go. When you take your kids shopping, they want *everything* and you end up buying *something*. They are good negotiators.

6. **Split-the-difference strategy.** If you give something, always try to get something in return. "If I do that for you, what will you do for me?" Never take the first offer, but always leave a little bit on the table. Never make a take-it-or-leave-it offer. Ask a question like, "How much better do I have to do to get an agreement with you? What must I do to get your approval on this?"

7. **The good-cop/bad-cop solo.** Know your bottom line, how much you are willing to concede, and then play both roles in a negotiating version of good cop/bad cop. The good salesperson says, "I like you and I want you to win," while the bad one reminds the prospect of the potential loss if you don't negotiate a favorable solution.

ANOTHER WIN-WIN STORY

Ron Willingham, the author of *The Best Seller*, tells how he sold the copyrights and inventory of a training program for $250,000. The terms were $25,000 down and $25,000 every six months until the balance was paid in full. Ron said that since the purchasing firm had a fairly low net worth but its president had a very high net worth, they negotiated an agreement that the president would sign the contract personally. However, when Ron received the contract it was not signed on the line that made the man individually, as well as corporately, responsible for the debt.

Ron contacted the president who said that he didn't want to sign it personally because that meant that his wife would be stuck with the debt if anything happened to him. Ron asked, "Is that the only reason you don't want to sign personally?"

The president assured him it was.

Ron said, "If I could guarantee that your wife would not be stuck with the debt, can we go forward with this agreement?"

The president said, "Yes."

Ron suggested that the president apply for a $250,000 term insurance policy that named Ron as the beneficiary. "I will pay the premiums on this policy until the note is paid in full. That way, if anything happens to you, the insurance company will pay the debt, and your wife will have no obligation."

This negotiation gave the president the safeguards he wanted, and Ron received a guarantee of payment for a relatively low cost.

FACING DOWN A PROFESSIONAL

Sometimes you will enter negotiations with a professional buyer. These people are usually in charge of all their company's acquisitions. Many of them have read all the books on negotiation and taken seminars as well. Their knowledge gives them power. When you are dealing with this type of buyer, it is important that you are perceived as having equal status.

Never be overly impressed by the buyer's power or fail to recognize your own power. If you have a good product or service, if it is one that will truly increase productivity, lower costs, affect employee morale, improve quality, give better service, or any one of a number of other advantages, you bring an equal position of power to the negotiation.

Homer Smith, in his book, *Selling Through Negotiation*, says that knowledge is power. "Knowledge about the product or service, its application to the prospects' needs or problems or wants, are sources of power for the salesperson.... Salespeople with regular customers are able to establish themselves as experts and become advisors and consultants to their customers on product selection and use. Salespeople calling on prospects rather than customers have to establish their credibility as advisors early, in order to get this power."

Good sales negotiators know that it is always better to do business in their own offices rather than the customer's. If possible, make customers come to you. Even more important, try to schedule the meeting when you feel and look good, when your emotions are up, and when the time is right.

The time is usually right when you don't need the deal. Whenever you can afford to walk away and you can convey that clearly to the prospective buyer, you are in a much more powerful position than if you go into the negotiation with hat in hand. On the other hand, you never want to seem arrogant about your use of power. Even when you are strongest (*especially* when you are strongest) let customers know you need their help. Ask them to treat you fairly.

Gather information without volunteering information. Information increases your power. Leaving things unsaid can be as important as saying the right things. Let the customers talk, rethinking their position aloud if necessary. Let them restate what they really want and modify their previous demands.

Watch their eyes. If their eyes start to wander, stop. Wait for them to process the information you've given them before you continue.

In fact, if the negotiations are not going well, try to stop the exchange altogether. Put it off until another time. When people have stopped listening or learning, or if they are feeling intimidated or fear they are losing control, they tune out. If you don't stop the discussion, you may break down the mutual trust and respect that is so important to win-win negotiations.

Roger Dawson maintains in his lectures and books that both sides can always win. In any negotiation, he says, the object is not to beat your opponent but to reach a creative agreement in which each negotiator can feel that he or she is the winner. Both sides can believe that they have cared about the other person's objectives, that they conducted their negotiations fairly, that they would like to deal with each other in the future, and that each party will keep the commitments they have made. This is truly connecting with your customer.

STEP EIGHT

USE TECHNOLOGY (IS THERE ANOTHER WAY TO DO THIS?)

Michelle Genovesi, a real estate agent, increased her income 30 percent over the previous year, a jump she attributes to having a notebook computer with her in the field. Michelle, who works with William Raveis Real Estate in Westport, Connecticut, says, "I can get great results by bringing my office with me. When I'm working with a home buyer, I can turn on my notebook, enter the customer's requirements, and up pops a detailed listing complete with pictures that I can print on my portable printer."

There are other ways of connecting with your customers besides meeting them in person. Good sales communicators take advantage of new technology to build bridges to their customers. Instead of resenting and rejecting technology, they use it to overcome barriers and create opportunities to serve customers better and gain a competitive edge.

Salespeople can connect with their customers by using letters, postcards, memos, faxes, newsletters, articles, voice mail, regular telephones, cellular telephones, electronic mail, answering machines, toll-free (800) numbers, pagers, audiotapes, videotapes, 35-mm slides, overhead projectors, presentation graphics, and all types of computers, among many other devices. Besides face-to-face presentations, good communicators master communication technology, from the common pencil to the most advanced computer system.

Although selling is one of the last parts of the corporation to become automated, sales automation is a booming industry. Technology is changing so rapidly that whatever I write today could be obsolete before this book is printed. However, it is safe to say that most salespeople will be using more and more automation in the years to come. The International Data Corporation has estimated that revenue from sales automation products will grow from $1 billion in 1994 to $2.7 billion by 1997, almost a 300-percent increase.

The size of technology is constantly shrinking, and most salespeople today can easily carry their offices with them. We have computers talking to computers, wireless phones, and e-mail. As the old saying goes, "You ain't seen nothing yet."

COMPUTERS

Today's salesperson can use computers for any number of tasks, including:

- Sales-cycle management
- Contact management
- Sales reporting
- Proposal generation
- Telemarketing
- Order fulfillment
- Customer support
- Promotion tracking

My friend David Arnold, Ph.D., writes and lectures on boosting business effectiveness by using Information Age tools and techniques. He stresses that a computer is more than a speedy address book, a high-tech adding machine, an advanced typewriter, or a more compact filing cabinet. It is a powerful tool for connecting with customers. According to Dave:

> You can build business relationships if you have a good contact-management software program. Graphics software is useful for illustrating your message by preparing handouts and effective slides for overhead projectors. A desktop publishing program is an easy way to produce brochures, flyers, and newsletters. And modems let us use our computers to increase the impact of telephone calls and faxes, E-mail and Internet.

Dave says that a computer can multiply marketing impact, increase sales, and help to deliver superior customer service when the sales communicator has the right hardware and software and learns how to use them correctly.

Small computers are called laptops, notebooks, tablets, palmtops or Personal Digital Assistants (PDAs). Laptops, notebooks, and palmtops have keyboards. Tablets and PDAs use an electronic stylus to control the computer. The latest PDAs can print, fax, and exchange information by modem. Their software includes a daily dairy, datebook, address book, and pocket versions of a financial database and a combination dictionary/thesaurus. All of this in the palm of your hand.

Tablets and PDAs are perfectly acceptable in meetings, but larger laptops and notebook computer screens are sometimes viewed as a barrier between the customer and the salesperson. I recommend sticking to the smallest device that will do what you need it to do. Some computer accessories are as small as a credit card. Today's wireless network cards connect you with a network, no matter where you are.

With the introduction of cellular digital pocket data and other wireless wide-area network definitions, salespeople will be able to stay in constant contact with their offices. There is even a tablet computer equipped with a cellular telephone. All these devices can help you take notes, retrieve information, and stay in touch with your office.

TELEPHONES

The telephone is one of the greatest sales tools. It comes with dozens of features to make selling easier, including call waiting, conference calling, and phone cards. Soon, we will each have a single phone number that can travel with us wherever we go.

Cellular telephones have replaced briefcases as the standard attachment to a salesperson's arm. Pagers are clipped to every man's belt and woman's handbag. Today's pagers are a far cry from the beepers of the past. Some can receive messages as well as phone numbers. Phones and pagers can speed your responsiveness to your customer, but they must be used efficiently. The following list provides some tips for ways to use these devices effectively.

1. **Organize your phone time.** Schedule a regular time to make your telephone calls. Start when you say you'll start and end when you say you'll end. Use telephone calls to replace some of your letters; a call can be more effective, faster, and cheaper than a letter. You can also use the telephone to replace many short meetings. (Every salesperson knows that we have too many meetings, so the phone can save a lot of time.)

2. **Plan your calls in advance.** What questions are you going to ask? Be ready to adapt your presentation to the customer's needs and time frames. This takes some research and preparation on your part, but it's worth it.

3. **Talk to the right person.** When you use the phone to set up appointments, a major concern is getting through to the buying authority. You don't want to waste time talking to people who are not decision makers. If someone blocks your way, use that magic question: "Can you help me?" Try to get the intermediary on your side. You can also send written information, ask the intermediary to put it in front of the

decision maker, and then make you an appointment for a follow-up call.

4. **Find out if the prospect can talk now.** Courtesy and good business tactics suggest that you make sure the person has time to listen before continuing the call. When you talk to a key person, always have two alternate presentations ready, a one-minute and a five-minute version, both filled with personal benefits. On the telephone you do not have time to go through all the rapport-building and fact-finding steps you would use during an in-person sales call. If you only have that all important single minute, you can still prepare a powerful presentation.

5. **Keep an accurate record.** Take notes of who you called, when, and what was said. You have no idea how valuable this can be for future reference.

6. **Don't give too much away.** If the purpose of your call is to arrange a meeting, you can undermine your personal presentation by leaking too much information on the phone. Save your punch line for the face-to-face encounter.

7. **Phone advantages.** Use the phone for:
   - Making appointments (if your purpose is to sell an appointment, don't try to do anything else).
   - Qualifying leads (it can save you lots of time in the long run).
   - Answering simple questions (you don't want to tell too much over the telephone).

8. Phone disadvantages. Don't use the phone for:

- Complicated proposals, products, or services (you won't be able to explain adequately). Use the phone only to initiate contact.
- Selling high-ticket items (few people will make a substantial investment over the phone).
- Anything that requires visualization, such as blueprints, charts, or graphs.
- Anything that requires hands-on use or demonstration, such as innovative tools or pieces of equipment.
- Closing a sale, unless your product or service calls for a very simple buying decision.

9. Follow through. This is the mark of a true professional. Anytime you talk to a customer or prospect, even if the person does not buy from you, write them a short note, just two or three lines, thanking them for their time.

PHONE AIDS

Computer programs like Telemagic, Ask, and ProSell remind you to follow through with your phone calls. These systems help control the sales process and can be very effective, but discipline yourself so the system doesn't become a crutch or a replacement for initiative and responsiveness.

Some salespeople like to use outside telemarketers, but most do their own telephoning.

TOLL-FREE TELEPHONE NUMBERS

If you work for a company that doesn't provide you with an 800-number, you should probably get one for yourself. You can order your own toll-free service by calling any of the several long-distance companies. Personally, I've found that an 800-number increases the number of customer responses by at least 50 percent.

Advantages of Having a Toll-free Number include the following:

1. Toll-free numbers encourage impulse buying.
2. Toll-free numbers let customers know you are open to their feedback.
3. These numbers make it more convenient for customers to place orders.
4. They shorten response time.
5. Toll-free numbers allow you to interact with your customers and offer better customer service.

Be sure your customers know about your 800-number. Put it on your letterhead, business cards, order forms, advertisements, and sales literature.

VOICE MAIL

In today's world, few people can take all their calls, and many business contacts end up on voice mail. This can be a serious obstacle to good sales communication. Using voice mail to your advantage starts with leaving the right message, one that is 30 seconds or less.

At the beginning of your message, give a good reason for the recipient to return your call, then give your name and telephone number. Be sure to do this at the *end* of your message, not the beginning. Then repeat your phone number.

Each week I telephone about 40 people, trying to sell my services as a speaker and trainer. For at least 30 of these people, I must leave a message on voice mail. This is what I usually say:

> *How can I fit into your process of communication and not be a pest? I'm really sorry that I couldn't speak to you personally today. I know you're busy. Will you please call me at 1-800-548-8001 and tell me how we can best communicate? This is Bill Bethel, and my phone number is 1-800-548-8001.*

This message is almost exactly 30 seconds, and it is the most effective message I've found for getting people to return the call. You'll notice that I did not give a brief sales talk. I simply said that I wanted to fit into their process of communicating, and would they please phone me and tell me how to do that.

AUDIOTAPES

Some salespeople mail 15- to 30-minute audiotapes to their customers to tell their sales story. A few years ago I created an audio tape for a company that was soliciting prospects for real estate investments, in both equity and mortgage loans. The first side was 20 minutes long and was called, "The Principles of Making Money Today." The company was never mentioned. This information was simply a shortened version of my four-hour talk on "Money: How to Get It, Keep It, and Make It Grow." The reverse side of the tape was a 20-minute commercial for my client.

The client ran small ads in newspapers throughout California, offering a free audiotape on how to make money. People who requested the tape received a follow-up phone call or a personal visit by a salesperson. This was the only prospecting method the company used for two years, and it kept their salespeople very busy.

VIDEOTAPES

Many sales professionals send a videotape to introduce themselves and their product or new idea. Recently I suggested that one company use a videotape as a prospecting device. They sent the video with an accompanying letter explaining that, since the tape was expensive to produce, their salesperson would come by to pick it up in a few days so they could recycle it. The salespeople were amazed at how many people saw them, returned the tape, and listened to additional information.

General Motors, like most car companies, has videotapes available for their salespeople to use as prospecting tools. One salesperson I know in the Los Angeles area buys mailing lists of prospects from a broker. These prospects are male, aged 25 to 40, earning incomes over $30,000 per year, and, according to car registrations, owning cars that are at least three years old. Then he selects 100 prospects each month and mails each of them a videotape. Three evenings a week, he shows up at the doors of those prospects. He introduces himself, asks if they received the tape, if they have had a chance to look at it, and if they'd like to take a demonstration drive: "The car is right out in front." Almost no one takes a drive immediately, he says, but eventually he get an amazingly high number of new car sales with this method.

FAXES

When it positively, absolutely, has to be there now, fax it. Faxes have become the bread and butter of business because contracts, proposals, confirmations, price lists, schedules, plans, and diagrams can be exchanged in seconds.

A fax is also a fabulous sales tool because it seems important. Faxes are usually read sooner and more completely than letters. For a long time, I fought purchasing a fax machine because I just couldn't see the benefits. Now I wouldn't be without it.

One of my favorite uses is following up when people don't return my phone calls. Sometimes I think about sending something like this:

> *If you wish to communicate, get in touch and we can talk about making the necessary arrangements to plan a discussion regarding the feasibility of some meaningful interpersonal dialogue leading to the possibility of organizing an ongoing purposeful conversation. In other words, please call me.*

Actually, I have never sent that. What I really say is:

> *You are a very busy person. I've been trying to get in touch with you. Can you call me Tuesday on my 800 number?*

This fax usually gets a favorable response.

FAX FACTS

- Keep your fax short. Say all you need to say, but make it more like a note or a memo than a letter. If it takes two pages, use two pages, but the shorter the better.

- Put technical and background information on separate pages. If it's not an absolute rush, send those separate pages by mail or overnight delivery. An initial-contact fax should simply explain that important information is coming.
- The more readable your fax is, the better. Use lots of white space, short paragraphs, simple words, and vivid benefits.

Using available technology can make you a more effective sales communicator. The days when all you needed were a sharp pencil and a yellow pad are gone. The complexity of our economy, the advances of technology, downsizing, and competition mean you must master every device you have available to make you an effective communicator for the twenty-first century.

STEP NINE

USE BODY LANGUAGE (WHAT SILENT MESSAGES ARE YOU SENDING?)

Keep your eyes on the road,
Your shoulder to the wheel,
Your ear to the ground,
And your nose to the grindstone.
(Then try to work in that position.)

The other day I went into a bakery and asked the salesperson which cake she would recommend. She was an absolute genius at body language, at expressing her feelings without words. Very carefully she looked over every cake in the store. She would start to move toward one, then shake her head and hesitate, then continue to search. Finally, her face broke into an enthusiastic smile. She reached into the case and pulled out a cake: "I think this one is just right for you." Could I argue? Of course not. Her body language had already convinced me that I was someone special and that she was making the most important selection of the day just for me.

There are two parts to communication. I call them the Two V's — vocal and visual.

- **Vocal communication** is what is said, how it is said, and how the words are interpreted.
- **Visual communication** is what is seen and how it is interpreted.

Gift Wrapping Yourself

Everything you say and do communicates something to your listener. Albert Mehrabian, a psychologist and researcher in behavioral science, says that 55 percent of all communication comes from facial and body expressions. We all know how important words and tone of voice are to communication. But most communication takes place not through what we say but through what we show. The more impressively a present is wrapped, the more impressive the gift.

Even experienced selling professionals sometimes forget that part of effective sales communication is how you present yourself. Do you show enthusiasm, confidence, and tact? What does your personal appearance say? First impressions are hard to overcome. The way you choose to package yourself is an important part of connecting with others.

This doesn't mean you have to look like a film star. You can be big, small, tall, or short. Just use your physical attributes to the best advantage. Try not to seem tense, withdrawn, or meek. Show that you are calm, confident, and in control. Your body language affects your customers.

The way you look also sends a subliminal message. No matter how long you've been in sales, check yourself carefully every day to decide what impression you're making. Wear clothes that are in style and fit well, but don't call attention to themselves. Avoid "gilding the lily" with excessive jewelry or adornments. Some people have strong, often unvoiced, prejudices against certain styles of dress, and these feelings may influence their decisions.

A QUESTION OF IMAGE

The thinnest briefcase I've ever seen was carried by Terry Gillis, a man who sold investments to pension fund managers. This case had room for only one folder. When I suggested he buy a larger one so he could call on three or four customers without replenishing his supply of handouts, he told me quietly that I had missed the point: "Big, bulky briefcases are for people who do the work. I want to create the impression that I am an idea man." He opened his briefcase and showed me the single folder. Written across it in large letters was:

> *"CONFIDENTIAL: For Your Eyes Only*
> *Especially prepared for (prospective client's name)"*

This, Terry explained, created the impression that no one was more important than this particular customer. With a silent, visual image, he showed that he had put in a great deal of time preparing for the interview. It must have worked because Terry was the top salesperson in his company.

YOUR BODY LANGUAGE

There are many nonverbal actions that influence potential customers. Smiles, facial expressions, hand gestures, body movements, head shaking, shoulder shrugging, fidgeting, and how you stand, walk, and sit all instigate responses in the viewer. Body language has been called the *silent language*.

Of course, you prepare your presentation carefully, making sure your voice is bright and friendly, and your words well chosen. Your next step is to decide what your body language says about you.

Sometimes you use nonverbal language without being aware of it. Unconscious gestures may convey messages you should keep to yourself. Does it show when you're tired, bored, or irritated? You've heard the term "poker-faced." Sometimes that expression is needed to keep others from knowing your emotions.

Do you have any nervous habits that may irritate others? For example, do you glance away a lot when you are talking to a customer? Some people consider this "shifty-eyed," indicating that the speaker is untrustworthy or has something to hide. This is especially true in traditional selling situations where most people maintain direct and extended eye contact. Americans are taught eye contact from childhood. When we glance away too frequently, we close communication.

Practice in front of a mirror or videotape yourself in action. Try to observe yourself objectively. Do you see any unconscious mannerisms that signal uneasiness? If these movements bother you on the tape, imagine how they affect your prospects or customers in person. Work on eliminating any nervous gestures and habits, the twitches and glitches that convey nothing but impatience, anxiety, or doubt.

The greatest sales communicators all have had their own unique gestures and expressions. Develop mannerisms that feel right for you, express your feelings positively, and bring positive reactions from your customers.

OTHER PEOPLE'S BODY LANGUAGE

Salespeople need to be students of behavior. Examine people. Remember the three kinds of knowledge that every good sales communicator must have: knowledge of people, product, and the process or techniques of salesmanship. I believe that people knowledge is the most important. When we study others, we learn about ourselves.

How do good sales communicators learn about people? They study. They spend as much time as possible with people in business and social situations, and they watch people everywhere—on busy streets, at bus stops and at airports, even in phone booths. They watch actors on TV with the sound turned off. What can that teach us about nonverbal communication? When we learn to read body language, we're better able to recognize the silent buying signals that our prospective customers are giving us.

People who are thinking things over sometimes shift position or walk around. They may clean their glasses, peek over the tops of their lenses, or stroke their chins. People who are involved lean forward; those who want to distance themselves lean back. If they're defensive, hostile, or doubtful, you'll find their arms crossed on their chest or their legs crossed.

When they don't understand or are doubtful or frustrated, they may run their fingers through their hair or rub the backs of their necks. Eye rubbing can mean "I don't like what I'm seeing." People who are bored or impatient may drum their fingers, swing their feet, look at their watches, or swivel their body so it aims toward an exit.

People who feel very confident, who perhaps see themselves in a dominant position in the exchange, may make a steeple of their fingers or grip their jacket lapels or cross their arms behind their back.

Remember that none of these signs is foolproof. They are only clues.

THE LANGUAGE OF FACES

Let your face know how you feel. The most expressive part of the body is the face. When we talk to people, we give their faces the most attention. Smiles indicate good will in almost every culture. Americans generally smile very freely. When your customer smiles at you, you can assume you are connecting with him or her.

Widened eyes indicate amazement, narrowed eyes hint at skepticism, and closed eyes mean we're thinking the situation over ... or that we've fallen asleep. A raised eyebrow, a slight frown, or a half-smile can speak volumes.

Among southern European and some Hispanic cultures, an animated face is considered appropriate and desirable at most times. Some Asians, on the other hand, tend to have less readable facial expressions.

THE LANGUAGE OF GESTURES

Gestures can speak loudly. Did you ever watch a military policeman directing traffic, a famous conductor leading an orchestra, or a baseball player protesting an umpire's decision? Each is a wordless essay and a learning experience for an astute communicator.

Can you learn to say something without using words? How about thumbs up, thumbs down, a shrug, a wink, a shake of the head, or a nod? Put up one finger. Which finger you choose says an awful lot about what you mean.

Don't evaluate a single gesture and assume you have grasped the full meaning. Consider every gesture in the context of what is going on around you. To hold up your index finger at a sporting event means you think your team is number one. Holding up the index finger when you enter a crowded American restaurant may mean a party of one. In Europe, raising a single index finger can be a rude gesture; someone dining alone holds up the thumb, while twosomes are indicated by thumb and index finger making an "L." Consider the total message in context.

Gestures across cultures should be approached carefully. The same gesture can have different meanings in different cultures. When former president George Bush visited Australia, it was reported worldwide that he had made an obscene gesture at some demonstrators. He maintained that he had given the "V for Victory" gesture, but with the back of his hand outward, index and middle fingers together, arm rising. In Australia, Britain, and most former British colonies, this gesture equals a raised middle finger in the United States. When Churchill first introduced the "V for Victory" sign in World War II, he undoubtedly intended it as a rude response to Hitler, but he modified this traditional obscenity by turning his palm outward, separating his fingers, and holding his arm steady.

In much of the world, an outstretched thumb means that you are hitchhiking, but in Australia, Turkey, or Bangladesh, it is an obscene gesture. Just to confuse you further, the Brazilians use this thumb gesture to mean "good luck."

The "okay" sign we use here in the United States to show approval—thumb and forefinger forming an "O"— is extremely obscene in Italy, Egypt, and the Middle East, indicating a bodily orifice and implying what you can do with it. This gesture is also rude in Greece and Russia, and indecent in Brazil, but in Japan it means "money."

If you happen to be speaking to a Fijian, don't fold your arms. That conveys disrespect. And if you exchange an object, such as a business card, with an Asian, present it or receive it with both hands to indicate respect.

Many of us talk with our hands. My wife used to say that if someone tied my hands behind my back, I'd be tongue-tied as well. Most Americans use moderate hand gestures, while immigrants from Italy, France, or Greece tend to gesture much more. Most Asian groups use very few hand gestures and keep their hands near their sides. In general, if you are talking to someone whose body language is more expressive and outgoing than yours, it isn't necessary to match it. However, if you are speaking with someone who is more restrained, tone down your own gestures. Most of all, show that you are trying to connect. Mistakes are easily forgiven when the message is sent that you care enough to try to adapt your behavior.

THE POWER OF SHAKING HANDS

A firm handshake has always been the hallmark of good salespeople, but it doesn't always translate across culture lines. Professionals take care not to impose their own idea of a good handshake. They let the customer set the tone.

In some cultures, handshakes aren't generally used. People in India place their hands, palms together, chest high, and make a slight bow. People from the Middle East use their right hand sweeping upward to touch their hearts, lips, and foreheads. The Japanese bow slightly, arms at their sides, to show respect. But Western customs have invaded most business situations. In modern Japanese offices, employees shake the boss's hand every morning on arrival and every evening before departure.

In America, we tend to shake hands when we are first introduced, when we arrive for and depart from a meeting, or when we encounter each other after some time has elapsed. We rarely shake hands with people whom we see everyday. But in France, you shakes everyone's hand on arrival and departure, even if the person is well known to you. Attending a meeting or social gathering with a dozen French people involves several minutes of hand shaking both coming and going (plus one, two, three, or four kisses on the cheeks of those with special claims of friendship or kinship). To communicate effectively, be sensitive to the wishes, customs, and comfort of your customer. Be ready to offer an American-style handshake, but never impose it.

SET THE STAGE

If your manner, posture, clothes, and grooming can give people silent messages about you, so can the things you surround yourself with. My friend, Walter Falk, owner of the Metropolitan Mortgage Company in Florida, has covered the wall of his office with the plaques, certificates, and awards he has received over the years for his business and community activities. When visitors to his office sit looking at those awards, how can they doubt that Walter is trustworthy, respected, admired, and a consistently active and involved member of the community?

Walter has another nonverbal technique that he uses to connect with his customer. Part of his office is furnished as a living room with a couch, an armchair, and a coffee table. Whenever Walter is with customers, he comes around his desk and sits in the armchair, leaving the couch for the customers. This creates a friendly and intimate feeling, as if he has invited them into his home. Walter always serves coffee or tea to prospective clients before he begins the business discussion. So there they are, sitting on a comfortable couch, looking over Walter's shoulder at a wall full of plaques and awards, drinking coffee, and discussing the benefits they will receive by doing business with Walter Falk. It's a powerful combination.

Whenever possible, don't put a barrier between you and your customer. A desk, a railing, a counter sends a message that is very clear: You are separate from your customer. Whenever possible, walk around the barrier and meet the customer as an equal. This is especially true when you are handling an unhappy or dissatisfied customer. Break down the barriers and connect.

When you seat people, position them in a triangle or "L" shape. In the latter grouping, sit on the shortest leg of the "L" and put the customers on the long leg, for example, a couch at right angles to a chair.

If you're seated at a table with a large group, try to sit at the head with prospects on either side. This lets you maintain good eye contact while you observe their body language. Round tables are even better, allowing interaction between all parties.

While we're on the subject of tables, lunch is an excellent place to connect with your customer. If you can find a quiet restaurant with soft background music, prospects will be more relaxed. Again, get L-shaped seating if possible, and allow the prospects to sit with their backs against the wall. They will feel "protected" and be better able to focus on you.

LAST-RESORT SIGN LANGUAGE

Gestures can save you when you don't speak another's language fluently. I speak no German, French, or Polish, so when I am in Germany, France, or Poland, I use gestures to try to indicate what I want. Once I walked up to a hotel desk and pantomimed my need to sleep by putting the palms of my hands together, laying them next to my cheek, closing my eyes, and tipping my head to one side. And, I got the room.

Many times I've pointed to food on someone else's plate and then to myself to order food. "Gesture-speak" may seem unnecessary when you are selling within the United States, but keep it in mind as a backup when you want to connect with someone who isn't proficient in the language(s) you speak.

READING AND WRITING SILENT LANGUAGE

It can be tempting to read too much into casual gestures. If people scratch their heads, they may have an itch, not an idea. If they cross their arms, they may be cold, not confrontational. A frown may be the result of eyestrain, a grimace the consequence of arthritis or tight shoes. Consider the total gesture package—posture, energy level, movement, position in relation to you—not just one gesture.

Body language shows how people feel about what they are saying. If words and movement don't match, always believe body language over spoken language. Reading bodily clues makes you more perceptive. It's what is sometimes called "intuition." When you have a gut feeling that someone isn't leveling with you, this usually means that their verbal and nonverbal messages don't agree.

There are many helpful books on body language, but I don't feel I have to study pictures 30 minutes a day to understand what each movement, gesture, or facial expression means. If people smile at me in a friendly way, I assume they like me or what I said. If they nod their heads, I assume this means yes. If they shake their heads, I assume it means no. (Of course, nodding the head up and down means no in traditional Chinese culture, and I'll remember that when I'm in China.)

Ultimately we communicate most by what we do. Example is always better than explanation. We can explain and explain, but unless our actions are in harmony with our words, we can't communicate our message. Emerson said, "What you do speaks so loud, I cannot hear what you say." So when you wish to really connect with your customer, be sure that what you do matches what you say.

STEP TEN

USE SELF-TALK (HOW DO YOU COMMUNICATE WITH YOURSELF?)

Life's battles don't always go
To the stronger or faster man,
But sooner or later the man who wins
Is the man who thinks he can.

       Napoleon Hill, The Law of Success

Whenever you're thinking, you're talking to yourself. The messages that you send yourself direct your behavior, habits, beliefs, and actions.

When you communicate with yourself, it's called *self-talk*. In the middle of the night when nobody's around, you express your real values, ethics, and goals. What you say to yourself is more important than all the words you say to others. What you say determines who you are, and who you are is the basis for connecting with your customers.

The chances are you talk to yourself quite often—in front of the mirror in the morning, driving, waiting in line, staring out the window, and at night just before you fall asleep. Your self-talk can be an internal monologue or an imagined dialogue with others. It can be positive or negative, and it can warn you, inspire you, or cause you worry. When you engage in negative self-talk, your mental computer acts on these messages and you'll set up a cycle of negative self-programming without even being aware of it. That's why it is so important to guard your mind. Every thought you think and every image you imagine contributes to faith or fear. You can strengthen your faith that people will like you, accept you, and contribute to your success. Or you can strengthen your fear that the opposite will be true.

Are you clear on who you are? Do you build a positive self-image and reinforce it over and over again? Do you have self-awareness and self-acceptance? The surest power we have is the power to present specific words, symbols, and images to our minds. The surest choice we have is the choice of what to think.

YOUR CHOICES

Many people wait to act until they must. When you recognize that you have choices, you free yourself to act because you want to, not because you have to. You can choose to listen, ask, speak, and connect.

Everybody is created equal. We all have 168 hours in every week. What makes us unequal is how we choose to use those hours. We choose what to say to ourselves, what to think and feel. Our self-dreams are the real reality. Which do you choose—limits or infinity? Words are the symbols with which we think, and thinking is silent speech. Thinking and communication are interdependent. The more clearly we think, the better we can communicate. The clearer our communication, the better we think.

Choices can be hard work when they require change. Tolstoi said that everyone thinks of changing humanity but no one thinks of changing himself. All successful salespeople know that for things to change, *they* must change. They must choose to trade negative and unproductive belief systems, self-talk, and visualizations for positive ones. They must think and act differently in order to be different. I believe that success is ultimately the result of intelligent effort, not lucky breaks, and that life is truly a bank account: If you don't put something in, you can't take anything out.

FIND YOUR MOTIVATIONS

You will never really connect with your customers if any of the following are true:

- You believe selling is somehow beneath you.
- You feel that successful selling is really beyond your capabilities.
- You suffer from a success block.

How do the attitudes of your friends and family influence you? Do your unconscious beliefs and attitudes write a self-fulfilling scenario?

Ask yourself, "What motivates me?" Decide what supplies your gas and what puts on your brakes. Are you excited about making lots of money? Is your goal financial security? Or would you love your job even if you had to pay to do it? How important is self-fulfillment to you? Do you want to be recognized as an achiever? Do you enjoy praise? Do you *need* praise? Do incentive awards, bonuses, or trophies put you in high gear? Is competition what revs up your engine? Are you challenged by setbacks? Does a turndown get your adrenaline going, or does it crush you, leaving you confused, depressed, and immobile?

When I first started in sales, one of my bosses discovered that I doubled or tripled my sales volume whenever I had a sales trainee in tow. My motivation, although I didn't realize it at the time, was that I had to impress these newcomers with how smart I was. Their amazement and awe was worth 10 times any extra commissions I earned.

Discovering and understanding your own personal motivations are essential to connecting with your customers. You have the power to shape and focus your motivations when you visualize, that is, consciously select the mental pictures and words you use.

The philosopher Schopenhauer said, "We seldom think of what we have, but always of what we lack." I hope in your case he's wrong. Visualization means turning the negative image of something you lack into a positive expectation of achievement. In the big picture of life, we inevitably get exactly what we expect to get. I've yet to meet anyone who has consistently exceeded his or her own expectations.

Good communicators have first-class expectations. In the Broadway musical, *How to Succeed in Business Without Really Trying*, the hero looks at himself in a mirror and sings, "I Believe In You." It is meant to be a satirical song, but when I saw that scene, it had a tremendous impact on my life. For the first time, I realized that I did believe in me. I had always told myself that I could succeed, and, step by step, little by little, I did.

When we don't have a program of self-talk focused on clear goals, we are like ships without fuel, drifting back and forth. Self-talk charts a course and fires the engines. Positive self-talk moves you toward your goals and encourages you to change unproductive habits. When we repeatedly tell ourselves that we will connect with our customers, we connect.

Self-talk builds self-image, and self-image is the key to all behavior. It determines how we react in any situation. It defines what we will and will not do, just as customers' self-images define what they will and will not do. Self-image is like a photograph. It lets us see ourselves, but it's a mental, not a physical, portrait. On the positive side, self-image motivates us. On the negative side, it sets our limitations. It's both our spur and our bridle, an accelerator and a brake.

USE VISUALIZATION

Every good salesperson has heard of positive visualization. With this technique, you use your imagination to visualize the results you want to achieve. You create a vivid image of how you will feel when you achieve that big sale, of the bounce in your step and the gleam in your eyes. You imagine the words you will use to brag to your boss, coworkers, and family. You plan how you will spend the commission or the big bonus.

My experience has taught me that we get exactly what we expect to get. Predictions of failure are always successful. When we focus on negatives, listening to the bad news about the economy, the recession in our industry, or the sales slump we find ourselves in, then we are sure to get more of the same. But when we concentrate on positive images, we inevitably advance.

Sending messages to your brain involves a delicate balance of emotional and intellectual input. Intellect can control negative emotional reactions, whereas positive emotions can overcome intellectual messages like, "It's never been done before" or "My chances of success in this situation are small."

Positive pictures are as important as positive words. Do you see yourself doing what you want to achieve and enjoying the results? For effective visualization, be selective about the images you create in your mind. "Futurize" in a positive manner.

Picture yourself reaching your goal. Don't concentrate on the steps involved. Instead, focus intensely on what it will be like when you have achieved what you want. Sometimes it helps to have real pictures as reminders. For example, collect photos of your role models or pictures cut from magazines and newspapers that relate to your goals. Put these images on the wall next to your bed or desk, in your locker at the gym, or inside a drawer where only you will see them. Use these images as constant reminders of where you are going.

Visualization is no longer considered pseudoscience. There are many documented cases of people who learn to do something successfully by practicing it over and over in their minds. Strong visualizations of goals and outcomes are not powerful in themselves, but because they energize and open the mind to opportunities and solutions that may have been overlooked. Obstacles that once would have been insurmountable suddenly become small inconveniences.

My wife Sheila used self-talk when she was just starting out in business. Things weren't going well for her, possibly because she was unclear on her goals and on what she wanted to achieve. A friend tried to stimulate her thinking by asking, "What do you wish you *didn't* have?" She decided that she really didn't want the battered, unreliable old car she was driving.

She visited new car showrooms, searching for her dream car. Finally she saw exactly what she wanted at British Motors: a burgundy TR-7. She ran over to the salesperson and said, "That's the car! That's what I want!"

The salesperson, whose name was Patrick, was as excited as she was. He got out his order pad. "No, wait," she said. "I need five brochures first." She explained that this car was going to be her goal. Patrick said, "Oh, no, another one of *those*!"

But Patrick gave her the five brochures. She taped one on the bathroom mirror so she had to peek around it in the morning to comb her hair. She taped the others on the refrigerator, the wall next to her desk, the inside flap of her briefcase, and the dashboard of her old car.

Once a week, Patrick telephoned her. "Hello, Sheila, how much money did you save this week?" When she could say "a lot," he'd cheer her. When she had to say "not so much," he'd encourage her.

A few months later she walked into the showroom and bought the car. She still has a photo of Patrick and herself with that car. This happened on a Friday. Early Sunday she was driving around the financial district of San Francisco. Like the financial district of every metropolitan city in the world on Sunday morning, it was absolutely deserted—no cars, no people, but lots of mirror-like plate glass windows along each side of the street. She could glance left or right and see a full-length reflection of herself driving down the street in her jazzy new car. Sheila had visualized herself into achieving her sales goals. She had used self-talk to energize herself to make the extra effort, to extend herself in uncomfortable and difficult situations so she would grow and learn to see disappointments and setbacks as challenges rather than failures. And Patrick believed in her and encouraged her self-talk.

USE ROLE MODELS

It helps to have a role model, someone you would like to emulate. Mentally practice being like this person. If you visualize yourself in this person's shoes, doing what he or she does, you offer yourself constant positive suggestions of what you want to become. Over time, your goals become your reality.

When I was starting out in sales, I had a powerful role model, a salesperson named Joe Bailey. Joe was everything I wanted to become. I came from a poor, uncultured home. Joe's family was wealthy, and he had attended very good schools in the east. I had little idea of fashion. Joe wore conservative, well-tailored clothes. I was easily derailed, but Joe, although he had an intensity about him, was always calm. Nothing ever ruffled or upset him, no matter what the circumstances. Joe was literally a tutor to me, teaching me selling, coaching me with math flash cards, advising me on what clothes to wear and what books to read.

Joe's primary focus was the welfare of his customers. We sold real estate, and I actually saw him turn down sales, telling people this deal wasn't for them. He literally wouldn't let them buy. I was young and inexperienced with no real principles to guide me. Watching Joe had a major impact on my life. I became the top salesperson for the company by patterning myself after Joe Bailey.

USE WRITTEN STATEMENTS

Another technique is to write down the words you want to live by. Be definite and specific. It is impossible to achieve something that's vague. One of the aids I use to stay positive is a simple 3″ x 5″ index card. On one side I've written my business philosophy, the rules that I will live by in business:

No hour is too early.

No hour is too late.

No distance is too far.

No amount is too small.

I've carried that card for years. Even though I know it by heart, I still take out that card and read it when I'm sitting in a coffee shop or at a traffic light. The physical act of seeing those words on paper helps keep this ideal ingrained in my mind. With this philosophy, I know it is almost impossible to fail.

On the other side of my card, I have my personal slogan. Everyone should have one, a short statement to repeat to yourself over and over. Mine says:

I will do what I do better and better and better, more and more and more.

In 1983, I read this sentence in a book by Eric Butterworth, a minister and author. It made sense to me then, and I can assure you that my life *has* gotten better and better and better and that I've had more and more and more.

Write down your personal and business philosophies and read them 10 times a day until they become second nature. Napoleon Hill, in his 1928 book, *The Law of Success,* said, "Habit is created by repeatedly directing your senses." Give yourself direction by reading your slogan over and over, preferably aloud. By using your sight and hearing, you make positive images into habits. Repeat your key phrases over and over. The more you repeat them, the more likely you are to remember the message you're sending yourself, and the more likely that message will have an impact on your actions. Once you've established habits, they will control and direct your actions, and your actions will control your results. You have created a constructive, positive cycle of autosuggestion.

Warning: Wishful thinking is not the same as autosuggestion. Thought can affect your results only if it is specific, focused, and intense. Be persistent in thinking positive thoughts, futurizing positive results, and acting as if it is impossible to fail.

In real life, negative input far outweighs positive input. Just read the front page of any newspaper or watch the nightly news. Our job is to overcome all the negativity that threatens us, to avoid it, ignore it, or convert it to positive challenges. There's a lively 1944 Johnny Mercer/Harold Arlen song that says, "Accentuate the positive. Eliminate the negative." That's still a good motto to live by.

Don't worry about the customer you lost. Concentrate on the next one you're going to sell. Use self-talk to open yourself to self-growth. Self-talk can fire your imagination and free your intuition. It can encourage you to accept refusals as opportunities to do better. It can even teach you to communicate better with your customers.

How badly do you want to learn to communicate? If your answer is that you really want to win at the selling game, you must erase and replace all your past negative programming. Eliminate the old and substitute new thought patterns and a new self-image. No matter what we have achieved in the past, every single one of us can do better.

Our first step is to reprogram our self-talk so we expect a higher level of achievement and act on that belief. Our ability to connect with others is an integral part of any achievement. When we are clear on the mission and purpose of our sales interviews, we are able to convince our customers of the benefits, both personal and financial, they can achieve. Our personal vision develops our negotiating ability, our persuasion techniques, and our willingness to ask for a commitment.

DEALING WITH REJECTION

Over the years one of my most successful activities has been selling to groups. Many firms, particularly investment companies, have hired me to conduct lectures or seminars where the primary purpose was to persuade an audience to buy a product.

One investment company booked me to give a talk aboard a cruise ship. I was selling an investment program with a 10-year lock-in provision, something with little appeal to anyone over 55 because older people want income, not long-term growth. Unfortunately the investment company hadn't checked to see who the passengers would be on this cruise.

When I walked out to give my presentation, I realized that there wasn't anyone under 65 in the room. There had been a special marketing program for senior citizens, and the average age on this cruise was over 70. Such an audience would have little, if any, interest in my product. However, since there wasn't much to do at sea, more than 100 people had turned up for my sales lecture.

My talk ended at noon, just as the gong sounded for lunch. You've never seen a room empty so fast! My reputation for closing a large percentage of my audiences took a terrible beating. On that occasion, I sold nobody.

Was this a personal rejection? Did they dislike me? Did they dislike my talk? Or was it possible that theirs was a simple business refusal caused by my offering a product that couldn't benefit them personally? And that their speedy departure was motivated by lunch, a personal benefit with which they could all identify?

When customers reject your product, they are not necessarily rejecting you personally. But if your self-image isn't strong and your confidence isn't high, you may decide that *you* are being rejected. Rejection can create negative mental pictures and thoughts. These thoughts may be expressed in the words you use to explain those pictures to yourself and others.

Strangers can't reject you, only your business proposition. For a refusal to affect you emotionally, you must have an emotional investment in the outcome. Of course, you care about your customers and your career, but a business rejection simply means that at this precise moment this customer does not want to buy this product or service from this salesperson. When you recognize this and refuse to take the rejection personally, you abort the cycle of negativity.

What you decide to do in any situation is consistent with the self-image created by your self-talk and personal vision. Your actions, positive or negative, constructive or destructive, will be consistent with how you perceive yourself.

I'm very fond of saying that everyone has the same feelings and emotional responses. If you insult me, I feel anger. That's an emotional reaction. I react emotionally, but I don't have to react physically. I can allow my intellect, self-talk, and thought processes to control my actions.

When you know you're okay, even if a prospect doesn't like your product, service, or the way you presented it, you can accept refusal and use it to grow. Each rejection helps you improve how you communicate the value of your proposition to others and to reinforce your belief in yourself.

It is good to realize that rejection is based on feelings rather than fact. Accept that you will undoubtedly have feelings, because self-talk must be emotional as well as intellectual. We must talk to ourselves on both an intellectual and an emotional level. You have choices about your emotional responses when you recognize that you alone control the images you create in your mind. When you change your pictures, you change your thoughts.

Years ago, I ran into the most protective guardian of a sales manager since the three-headed dog Cerberus sat at the gates of hell. Her name was Arlene. She was curt, surly, and extremely difficult. Few salespeople ever got past her. I had a great rapport with her boss, but that did me little good because it was nearly impossible to get in to see him. One day, I made a conscious decision to visualize Arlene as my ally. I smiled whenever I approached her, ignored her icy manner, and always responded as if she were being very friendly toward me. I came up with as many honest compliments as I could, saying things like,

"Gee, I wish I had a secretary as protective of me as you are of Mr. X." It took persistence and enormous mental effort, but it worked. Eventually Arlene became one of my greatest allies and referred lots of business to me.

DEALING WITH WORRY

For some people, worry becomes a magical force in their lives because every time they worry about something, that thing never happens. They decide that if they just keep worrying, they can protect themselves from future calamities.

Worry is a sign of fear, often fear of success or fear of failure. We have programmed ourselves with self-talk so that when unpleasant situations from the past are repeated, we feel fear. Maybe we were criticized by parents, teachers, or friends. They said, "Don't do that. Don't try. If you do, you'll fail." Those old mental tapes play over and over in our heads. "What is Mom going to think of me?" "What is Dad going to think of me?" "What is the teacher going to think of me?" "What is my spouse going to say?" "What is my neighbor going to say?" "What is my boss going to say?" Let me tell you a secret: All these people are so concerned about what other people think of them they rarely think anything about you.

If you want to increase your self-esteem and self-confidence, change your self-talk. Don't be afraid of failing or succeeding. If you absolutely have to worry, worry about the chances you'll miss when worry keeps you from trying. Remind yourself that you are a unique human being and that you deserve all the success you can earn. That's the key word: *earn*. Success can't be borrowed, stolen, demanded, or faked for very long. True success is earned, and earned success is never lost.

DEALING WITH PAIN

Most of us have developed our self-image by trial and error. We try, we fail, and we try again. Success is often preceded by ridicule, pain, and humiliation. Despite ultimate success, these failures stay in our unconscious memories. Our subconscious minds continue to dredge these unpleasant experiences.

Sometimes we avoid trying something difficult so we can avoid the discomfort of failure. Sometimes our self-talk tells us not to act at all. We end up avoiding the actions that lead to success because of negative messages our self-talk has programmed into our minds.

To overcome any negative messages still lurking in your mind, use the "Act as if" technique. Act as if it is impossible to fail. Act as if your communication skills are so advanced that you can influence and persuade your customers as easily as you influence and persuade yourself. Your positive self-talk becomes a self-fulfilling prophecy, and what you say to yourself becomes true. You get what you predict and believe.

How many times have you heard people say, "I ought to … " or "I should … "or "I could have … or "If I only … " From now on say, "I believe," "I can," and "I will."

MY OTHER ROLE MODEL

Whenever I feel like something can't be done, I think of my real-life business hero, Willy Durant. In 1886 he borrowed $2,000 from his friends and bought an interest in a carriage factory. Within four years he built the business into one of the largest carriage makers in the United States, producing 150,000 horse-drawn carriages a year.

But as we all know, horses were soon edged out by the automobile.

Everyone was telling Durant to get out of the business. Instead, he purchased the Flint Wagon Works in Michigan. He told everyone that this purchase was going to make him a fortune. He didn't know how, but he believed that he would find a way. Someone told him about a screwball inventor named David Buick who was experimenting with a piston engine. Willy Durant approached Mr. Buick and said, "Let's manufacture automobiles. I can make the carriages." They formed a partnership and renamed the company the Buick Motor Company.

Next, Durant started telling his friends that he was going to be the world's biggest automobile maker. He borrowed more money from banks, acquaintances, and family members. Then he added both Cadillac and Oldsmobile to his company, changing the name to General Motors. The banks that Durant had borrowed from decided he was too much of a dreamer, so they forced him out of his position as president of the company and put someone else in his place.

When Durant's friends offered sympathy, he told them the bankers had offered him the biggest opportunity of his life. He was going to locate another venture and make enough money to buy up controlling stock in General Motors.

One year later, he met a man named Lewis Chevrolet who had designed a low-priced car. Durant scraped together the money to start manufacturing. Just two years later, using the profits from Chevrolet, Willy Durant had purchased enough voting stock certificates to force the General Motors board of directors to put him back in control of the company. This was 1920, and his net worth was $105 million, all in GM stock. When someone asked him how he did it, Willy Durant said, "I just don't believe it's possible to fail if you continually remind yourself of your goals and keep working toward them."

Willy Durant acted as it were impossible to fail. He refused to fall into the "If only I … " trap.

THE POWER OF PROMISES

Professional salespeople have a reputation for doing what they should, when they should. Why? Because they've learned to motivate themselves as well as their clients.

When you do the right thing, it increases your self-esteem. When you make a promise and keep it, you feel good about yourself and boost your confidence level. When you make a promise and break it, you decrease your self-esteem. Make promises to yourself, your clients, your company, your industry, your community, and your family. Then keep every promise you make. Always do what makes you proud; never do what makes you ashamed of yourself.

BEING A PROFESSIONAL

Since medieval times there have been only four professions: law, medicine, religion, and higher academia. Their practitioners were called professionals because they had to profess or swear an oath. In more recent times, *professional* has come to mean "not an amateur." If you are paid, you are a professional. If you do something for free, you are an amateur.

Today, professionalism has another meaning. It's not the job you do, it's how you do the job. Being a professional sales communicator means that you project your vision, knowledge, drive, sensitivity, and nuts-and-bolts know-how into your customers' hearts and minds. It means you can understand intellectually and emotionally what your customers' needs, wants, and fears are. And it means that, through your superior communication skills, you can convince your customers that your product or service will solve their problems, fix what's wrong, and help them achieve their own goals. That's professional sales communication, and that is connecting with your customers.

Why do you talk to other human beings? With TV, radio, newspapers, magazines, billboards, and direct mail, what is the point of actually talking to a potential customer? The best advertising brains in the world constantly bombard the public with blaring and subliminal messages, moving billions of dollars in merchandise and services.

I still say that the best way to persuade is face to face, so people can see your eyes, hear your voice, and feel your presence. When they can experience and be excited by you and your product directly, they are more inclined to buy. No one knows what kind of mood a TV or newspaper ad will find potential customers in, or even if they will notice the ad. But when you're there in person, you are communicating on the hottest, most intense, primary level.

Advertising communicates to the average person and uses the lowest common denominator. Personal interaction puts you in control of the most sophisticated form of selling: one-on-one, dynamic communication. This is how to truly connect with your customers.

BIBLIOGRAPHY

Alessandra, Anthony J., and Phillip S. Wexler. *Non-Manipulative Selling*. Reston, VA: Reston Publishing, 1979.

Anderson, Karen. *Getting What You Want*. New York: Dutton, 1993.

Axtell, Roger E. *Gestures: The Do's and Taboos of Body Language Around the World*. New York; John Wiley & Sons, 1991.

Bagley, Dan S., III, and Edward J. Reese. *Beyond Selling*. Cupertino, CA: Meta Publications, 1987.

Bechler, Curt, and Richard L. Weaver II. *Listen to Win: A Manager's Guide to Effective Listening*. New York: MasterMedia Limited, 1994.

Beier, Dr. Ernst G., and Evans G. Valens. *People Reading.* New York: Stein and Day, 1975.

Dawson, Roger. *You Can Get Anything You Want.* Reprinted as *Secrets of Power Negotiating.* New York: Fireside Book, Simon & Schuster, 1985.

Elgin, Suzette Haden. *Genderspeak.* New York: John Wiley & Sons, 1993.

Fisher, Roger, and William Ury. *Getting to Yes.* New York: Penguin Books, 1981.

Hill, Napoleon. *The Law of Success.* Meriden, CT: Ralston University Press, 1928.

Hybels, Saundra, and Richard L. Weaver, II. *Communicating Effectively,* 2nd ed. New York: Random House, 1989.

Johnson, Kerry L. *Mastering the Game: The Human Edge in Sales and Marketing.* Louis & Ford Co., 1987.

Parinello, Anthony. *Selling to VITO.* Holbrook, MA: Bob Adams, Inc., 1994.

Pease, Allan. Signals: *How to Use Body Language for Power, Success and Love.* Toronto: Bantam Books, 1984.

Rackham, Neil. *Spin Selling.* New York: McGraw-Hill, 1988.

Richardson, Jerry, and Joel Margulis. *The Magic of Rapport.* San Francisco: Harbor Publishing (distributed by G. P. Putnam's Sons), 1981.

Ross, Percy. *Ask for the Moon — and Get It!* New York: G. P. Putnam's Sons, 1987.

Tannen, Deborah. *You Just Don't Understand: Women and Men in Conversation.* New York: Ballantine Books, 1990.

Thiederman, Sondra. *Profiting in America's Multicultural Marketplace.* New York: Lexington Books, 1991.

Tingley, Judith C. *Genderflex: Ending the Workplace War Between the Sexes.* Phoenix, AZ: Performance Improvement Pros, 1993.

Weaver, Richard L., III. *Understanding Interpersonal Communication,* 6th ed. New York: HarperCollins College Publishers, 1993.

Woolf, Bob. *Friendly Persuasion: My Life As a Negotiator.* New York: G. P. Putnam's Sons, 1990.

INDEX